Slow Journeys

Other books by Gillian Souter

Classic Walks in Western Europe
Walking France
Walking Italy

Slow Journeys

THE PLEASURES
OF TRAVELLING BY FOOT

GILLIAN SOUTER

ALLEN&UNWIN

First published in 2009

Allen & Unwin
83 Alexander Street
Crows Nest NSW 2065
Australia
Phone: (61 2) 8425 0100
Fax: (61 2) 9906 2218
Email: info@allenandunwin.com
Web: www.allenandunwin.com

Cataloguing-in-Publication details are available
from the National Library of Australia
www.librariesaustralia.nla.gov.au

ISBN 978 1 74175 965 5

Internal design by Emily O'Neill
Set in 11.5/16 pt Granjon by Bookhouse, Sydney
Printed and bound in Australia by Griffin Press

10 9 8 7 6 5 4 3 2 1

To John, for bearing more than just a backpack

CONTENTS

Preambling
...

Few men know how to take a walk. The qualifications . . .
are endurance, plain clothes, old shoes, an eye for nature,
good humour, vast curiosity, good speech, good silence
and nothing too much.
RALPH WALDO EMERSON, 1858

The working title of this volume was *Walk Walk Walk*. It held
appeal, partly because the thought of someone enquiring for
it at a bookshop honking like a goose amused me, but also because
I wanted to convey to potential readers that this would be a book
not merely on ambling or moseying about but on striding out with
purpose and a destination. Then I realised that no one likes to be
mistaken for a goose and, rather than risk the book remaining
unbought and unread, I had better spell out my intent in a subtitle.
So you are warned: when the term *walking* is used in this book, it
means covering a good distance over a series of days, with a view

to seeing the world. Your long walk may take you through your own neighbourhood or it may lead you further afield; exploring the world at walking pace is a wonderful form of slow travel. If you have limited time, the pleasures of even a few days spent walking with a destination in mind and a bit of decent weather are considerable.

For those in the know, there are books in abundance on hiking. If they are not about specific routes, they tend to include the words 'survival' and 'wilderness' in the title and are almost always written by men with beards. Such books are usually concerned with off-track walking: finding your own way across a landscape while being self-reliant for food and shelter. For some tough souls, this mode of walking is the option of choice—and it does have the obvious benefit of taking you places where few have been and where the environment is at its most pristine. But it also means you have to carry an awful lot and cope with whatever nature might throw at you, all the while eating some very mediocre meals. On a footpath, you can cover more distance and see a lot more of the landscape and less of the ground. Your path will pass by huts and hamlets where you'll be well fed and sheltered. Travelling on a durable path, you will do less damage to the environment you pass through. You will also do less damage to *you*: a path offers a route free of hazards such as thorns, vines and stinging nettles. I walk off-track in Australia with a local group of enthusiasts and the state of my legs attests to the injuries that cruel vegetation can inflict. Sword grass, needle bush and dagger hakea are well named!

There are generally good reasons that footpaths follow the route they do: a path may be the easiest route over a high mountain pass, or it may be an ancient right of way connecting villages via land that cannot be traversed by car. Footpaths are seldom direct lines from A to B: they are the negotiations of humans with the lie of the land. They may have been worn by the mules of traders and itinerant workers, or perhaps by the soles of pilgrim souls. Broader paths may be ancient droving roads used for the the movement of livestock up to summer pastures and back to winter shelter, or the routes of Roman legions defending far-flung provinces. Walking in the footsteps of others adds an extra dimension to your journey. Lastly, there are few things more pleasing to the eye than a narrow path winding o'er the brow of a hill; the very thought makes me come over all nostalgic. Such a path seems to draw the eye and beckon the viewer with the promise of a destination. For all of these reasons, this book does not concern itself with navigating a route off-track.

Increasingly, leisured societies are enjoying distance walking as a pastime. Australians *bushwalk* everywhere, even in desert and along beaches where there are no bushes. New Zealanders *tramp* and South Africans *trail*. Those in the United States *hike* or *backpack* (while backpackers elsewhere are travellers doing it cheap). The British used to *ramble*, but these days they're more likely to *hillwalk*, which is far more prosaic. Italians who are feeling energetic stretch the limbs for *quattro passi*. The French, in true Gallic style, have made walking an art form with numerous terms of discourse: *balade* for a short stroll, *tour* for a circuit, *grande randonnée* for a seriously long walk, and even a name—*flânerie*— for an amble undertaken with no particular destination but with an inquiring mind. According to the historian Simon Schama, the

French invented the waymarked leisure trail in 1835 or so, when Claude-François Denecourt splashed blue paint on trees to mark a ten-kilometre walk through the forest of Fontainebleau. He followed this up with four other routes, published a short guide noting points of interest, and so made popular the pastime of hiking. Within two decades, there were 150 kilometres of marked trails through that forest and thousands of citizens arrived each weekend to tread them. Fortunately, there are now more than 180,000 kilometres of waymarked paths crisscrossing France, so we don't have to bump into each other in Fontainebleau. Indeed, there are now blazed walking trails all over the world.

I am not alone in trying to share the pleasures of walking, and there are many fine essays that will do the job much more pithily. Following social convention, the joys you've experienced on a long-distance excursion have to be scattered frugally into various conversations over time. I'm personally fed up with waiting patiently for my turn to relate anecdotes, so here it is: a book that will deplete my cache of stories and force me to go in search of fresh ones.

A sensible reader might ask whether I am qualified for the task at hand. Perhaps: along with my map-loving partner, John, I have walked a great deal in Europe and Britain and a fair bit in New Zealand and Australia—and I am extremely opinionated, which is a good start. And there's the nub: walking isn't a science that requires years of study, or a craft that demands half a lifetime of apprenticeship. As Emerson realised, there are very few qualifications. It's simply a matter of putting on your old boots, hoisting your pack and heading off down that winding path.

1. Why walk far?
...

Apparently, some bystanders consider that 'just for pleasure' isn't sufficient reason to go on a long walk. Charles Konopa, an American hiker who encountered this attitude of suspicion too often, relates a delightful anecdote of a walker who felt obliged to carry a small flower press in his backpack. That way, when asked by people he met along the way, he could say that he was collecting plants. The 'plant collector' stumbled onto a genuine interest in flora and went on to become an expert botanist. Konopa, encouraged by this example, tells those who ask why he is hiking that he is testing trail footgear, which satisfies their curiosity.

ANCIENT FOOTPRINTS
I suppose the larger question is: why travel? Why leave home at all? Originally, there was no home to leave—hunters sought

seasonal hunting grounds, herders sought fresh pasture—and it wasn't until humans had to hang around for crops to grow that we began to settle down. Most of the race opted to stay put, and have been suspicious of those who constantly travel—such as the gypsies or Romany people—ever since. From time to time, though, there were reasons to leave the safety of the community. Bold individuals ventured out in search of materials and metals to enrich our lives, and others then travelled to trade these for further riches. On occasion, ransacking barbarians had us on the move. At other times *we* were the ransacking barbarians, moving into better neighbourhoods.

As humankind got organised and states expanded, officialdom had to get out and about to collect taxes, convey messages or act as envoys. If the latter didn't do their job properly, inevitably armies were dispatched to sort things out. Borders were breached by cunning smugglers, so customs officers patrolled remote coasts and mountains to catch them in the act. Even once we'd acquired enough goods, there were oracles to consult and shrines at which to worship. Relatives who'd married into other clans had to be visited, the sick sought cures and the wealthy travelled to enjoy health-inducing spas and to breathe sea or mountain air. If the therapy failed, you might have to make the journey along corpse roads to bury your dead in sanctified ground.

Don't imagine, though, that vast numbers were crisscrossing the countryside before someone came up with mechanised transport. Until relatively recently, travel was difficult and often dangerous: something to be endured rather than enjoyed. People who travelled without immediate purpose were rare; any such self-motivated travellers went in search of knowledge—specifically knowledge of human achievement and custom. Accounts of travel in the ancient world seldom bother to comment on the natural environment as a matter of interest in itself: terrain was either hospitable or impassable.

There were undoubtedly some souls who joined the Crusades or undertook pilgrimages for reasons other than to atone for crimes or earn heavenly bonus points: a trip to the Holy Land or to Canterbury was also a relatively safe and respectable way to get away from your suffocatingly tight community and go sightseeing. No one would admit this, though: when the concept of travel for its own sake arose, the stated object was to learn about other societies. Sir Francis Bacon, writing an essay on travel in 1625, lists a good half page of 'Things to be seene and observed', including the courts of princes, walls and fortifications of cities, arsenals and so on. Bacon even points out that 'such shows' as 'capital executions' should not be neglected. The closest thing on the list to nature, however, is 'gardens of state, and pleasure, neare great cities'. No majestic waterfalls or lofty, inspiring mountains but gardens: nature tamed and civilised.

A NATURAL AWAKENING

The appeal of the countryside apparently went largely unnoticed until a new romantic spirit arose in the late eighteenth century. The Romantics liked their Nature wild, perceiving that depictions of the untamed natural world could reflect and express our human emotions. What's more, the effort to experience it on foot (rather than on horseback or by carriage) was a stimulus to creativity.

According to poet William Wordsworth's sometime friend and tenant Thomas De Quincey, walking was a mode of exertion which, for Wordsworth, 'stood in the stead of wine, spirits and all other stimulants whatsoever to the animal spirits; to which he has been indebted for a life of undiluted happiness, and we for much of what is most excellent in his writings'. And this from a man who was himself addicted to laudanum. For these Romantic poets, walking wasn't merely a means to witness inspiring vistas; the very motion of perambulation aided creativity. Essayist William Hazlitt even suggested that the mode of walk affected poetic style:

> Coleridge's manner is more full, animated, and varied; Wordsworth's more equable, sustained, and internal. The one might be termed dramatic, the other more lyrical. Coleridge has told me that he himself liked to compose in walking over uneven ground, or breaking through the straggling branches of a copse-wood; whereas Wordsworth always wrote (if he could) walking up and down a straight gravel-walk . . .

And it's not just rhymes that those long walks inspired: in the nineteenth century the hills were full of prose writers as well. Thomas De Quincey was himself a keen walker, undertaking a 'pedestrian excursion' through Wales when he ran away from school at the age of sixteen. During his fortnight-long walk he saved on the cost of inns by bivouacking, making him a forerunner of backpackers. Hazlitt himself liked nothing better than 'a jaunt', walking for several days. Philosophers also appreciated the combination of a change of scene and physical exertion as an aid to thought. The lovely town of Heidelberg, where a school of the German Romantics flourished, still has a Philosophers' Walk or *Philosophenweg* that zigzags up one steep side of the valley. Mountaineering—which is essentially walking vertically—was developed by energetic young clerics, philosophers and artists seeking spiritual and aesthetic truth in the Alps. And it wasn't just a Western notion: Mount Fuji, Japan's highest mountain, was reputedly first climbed by a seventh-century monk, Enno Ozuno. For the less vertically minded, Kyoto has its own Philosophers' Walk, alongside a canal in the shade of cherry trees, where the attainment of enlightenment is a decidedly more tranquil affair.

FOR BODY AND SOUL

Whatever your creative aspirations, movement is undoubtedly a stimulus for a sound mental state. My partner, for example, can't stand in the one spot when something's perplexing him; I get dizzy watching. He has a good historical precedent for this involuntary motion: Aristotle found that pacing up and down aided him in philosophical debate—and the school he established in ancient Athens was nicknamed the Peripatetic School for just this reason. The French philosopher Jean-Jacques Rousseau went so far as to claim: 'I can only meditate when I am walking. When I stop, I cease to think; my mind works only with my legs.' Rousseau got his mental exercise outdoors, where he could also let nature take its effect. You might not be aiming to develop a revolutionary philosophy of life, but walking will certainly help you deal with your own concerns. On the path there's plenty of time for introspection, and it often happens that your problems are resolved, put into context, or dismissed altogether.

A long walk is also a great way to counter a lull in mood, or more serious depression—especially, it seems, for postmenopausal women. It may be due to simple body chemistry, but I doubt any amount of exercise in a gym will achieve quite the same effect. The composer Felix Mendelssohn, who for most of his life created light, cheery music as befitted his name, was beset by a terrible grief following the death of his sister Fanny in 1847. To salve his low spirits he travelled to the Bernese Alps in Switzerland, where he painted watercolours of the peaks and glacier-carved valleys and, by a contemporary's account, 'took to walking immoderately . . . he said it was the only thing that would calm his mind'. Along the way he composed the hauntingly beautiful *String Quartet in F minor*, so all that walking certainly did the rest of us some good—if not poor Felix, who died not long after from a paralytic stroke.

Religious pilgrims usually have a hallowed site as their destination, but it's the long walk to reach it that serves as the spiritual cleansing agent. I've never understood the appeal of meditative stillness. What's the point sitting around in a cave and meditating your way into mindlessness? To me, those out on the path—and it doesn't have to be the same one that everyone else is treading—are much further along the road to spiritual health. Reinhold Messner a contemporary mountaineer of renown, has said that long marches

> are the surest, if not the only, way to avoid spiritual blindness.
> They provide the possibility, or rather the necessity, of
> uniting the active and the contemplative components of

one's nature. This is never more easily achieved than on a long trek.

Sigmund Freud, the father of psychoanalysis, was an avid walker who was strongly drawn to mountain scenery. He considered his regular walking holidays in the Dachstein, the Tyrol, the Tatras and other massifs essential to his mental wellbeing and an integral part of his *Weltanschauung*, or philosophy of life.

Keeping the rest of the body fit is another benefit of distance walking, but to many it is merely incidental. (The footloose French-born writer Hilaire Belloc went so far as to claim that the 'detestable habit of walking for exercise' warps the soul.) Nonetheless, it's a bonus to find yourself willingly engaged in something that's good for you. First off, the clean air that hovers about in the countryside has got to be doing your lungs a favour. You're also helping to prevent high blood pressure, heart disease, osteoporosis, diabetes and bowel cancer while toning the legs, buttocks and stomach. A recent study even suggested that, for people over the age of fifty, walking helps prevent memory loss.

Walking is an activity that, unlike more taxing pursuits, can be continued into later age; we've met plenty of walkers on the track who have seen several more decades but can match us step for step. Having said that, wayfaring is not a competitive pastime. Distance walking can undoubtedly be a personal challenge and a test of both physical and mental endurance. It's something at which women, who are often strong in stamina rather than aerobic fitness, can excel: our usual pattern is that my partner

John pushes ahead on the steep hills but inevitably lags behind in the second half of the day. (For the record, John wishes to declare that he is five years older, with a history of dodgy lungs and a minor mitral valve leak—a legacy of open-heart surgery. Excuses, excuses!)

On a long walk, the body takes delight in being employed every day and falls into an easy, pleasurable rhythm. It also learns to walk efficiently, stepping more surely over difficult ground and allowing the mind to concentrate more fully on the surrounding sights and sounds. After several days on foot, you tune in more fully to the natural world and start to understand the shape of the land. On a very long walk, you begin to perceive how environments fit together along the ribbon of your route.

Walking is educative in the same manner as other forms of travel, although the syllabus is more often focused on natural history than on Bacon's social studies. It's unlikely in this day and age that you'll be covering fresh ground, and there is some pleasure and great interest to be gained from treading in other footsteps. History becomes tangible at this level, where you can discover how humankind has shaped the land or merely made a narrow incursion through it. Signs of early inhabitants or of pioneers are particularly exciting, but more recent predecessors are also interesting to follow, especially those who've written about their excursion. Scottish author Robert Louis Stevenson's *Travels with a Donkey in the Cévennes* describes a route that can still be followed over the Massif Central of France, where little has changed since his insights were penned in 1878. More and more young Australians are walking the Kokoda Trail in Papua

New Guinea, following the route of Australian soldiers and their local guides as they fought off invading Japanese troops during the Second World War. Sometimes, a long walk is a more personal journey: we recently walked through the Swiss Alps, staring up in amazement at pointy mountains my mother and father had crested some sixty years previously.

Everywhere you might walk has most likely been explored, mapped and described, but there's still the thrill of small discoveries. You may have flicked through lavishly illustrated books on a region or viewed David Attenborough's latest wildlife documentary, yet nothing will match your personal experience of walking through a landscape, with certain light and weather conditions at a particular time of day, or catching sight of a wild animal in its natural state. Such experiences are sublimely unmediated. A walk can take you to that place no car can reach, where animals can be surprised and vegetation is untrammelled. As a bonus, you can derive a degree of righteousness from the fact that careful walking is an environmentally healthy method of travel. Locals whom you meet appreciate your light-footed approach: walkers are far less obtrusive than busloads of visitors. Many also understand that you've done some hard work to get to their corner of the world, and your travails make you more of a traveller than a tourist. This shared toil also leads to a great sense of fellowship among walkers who meet on the path: you're unlikely to encounter deeper camaraderie anywhere else.

Robert Louis Stevenson counted himself among 'the brotherhood' of those who undertake walking tours. He went not 'in quest of the picturesque, but of certain jolly humours—of the hope and spirit with which the march begins at morning, and the peace and spiritual repletion of the evening's rest.' The sense of wellbeing as you roll along the path is a fine thing, but that feeling at day's end is hard to match. As Stevenson put it:

> If the evening be fine and warm, there is nothing better in life than to lounge before the inn door in the sunset, or lean over the parapet of the bridge, to watch the weeds and quick fishes. It is then, if ever, that you taste joviality to the full significance of that audacious word. Your muscles are so agreeably slack, you feel so clean and so strong and so idle, that whether you move or sit still, whatever you do is done with pride and a kingly sort of pleasure.

The satisfaction of completing a day's walk is only enhanced by the appetite it gives you for a hearty meal and a good bottle of red.

Long-distance walking compounds that sense of achievement. The destination takes on extra significance and you arrive at it with mixed feelings: thrilled to have reached your goal, but sorry to have ended the journey. Even on a short walk, it can be profoundly affecting to remove yourself from the trappings of civilisation and to experience and appreciate your place (or, in wilder regions, your lack of place) in the natural world. As philosopher Alain de Botton reminds us, our experiences in nature and the images that we store up can be a lasting resource to nourish the soul on later occasions. In these days of aggressive marketing, constant consumption and other social pressures associated with urban living, the soul could certainly do with a lot of nourishing. A journey on foot continues on in your memory long after you've completed it, like a river-polished stone that you can keep in your pocket and rub from time to time.

There are many motives for wayfaring. Stevenson's reveal the ascetic Scot in him:

> For my part, I travel not to go anywhere, but to go. I travel for travel's sake. The great affair is to move; to feel the needs and hitches of our life more nearly; to come down off this feather-bed of civilisation, and find the globe granite underfoot and strewn with cutting flints.

Being of Scottish birth myself, I can empathise with that desire to strip life down and take the road less comfortable. There is a simplicity and even a purity in distance walking that is, to me, irresistible. Your concerns are very immediate: where to collect water, which way to turn. You are at liberty to go as you please—you are footloose.

PERSONALLY SPEAKING

For me, walking has the added incentive of being an inexpensive means of travel: I was born in Aberdeen, after all. Both my parents were keen mountaineers and they met on the slopes of the Scottish Cairngorms, a bleak setting for most romances, but quite fitting for their no-nonsense partnership. They gave up mountain-climbing to raise children and took us walking instead. Once the family migrated to Australia, each holiday was spent exploring a different national park, most often on foot. I was the youngest child and no doubt cunning strategies were used to encourage me along the track. I was charged with responsibility for a little red rucksack with not a lot in it. Knowing my mother's hoarding proclivities, I suspect it's still tucked at the back of a high cupboard in the family home.

John, on the other hand, led an altogether different childhood. World-championship wrestling was the favourite weekend pastime for his male-dominated family, and appears to have been the only physical exertion undertaken in his youth: school sports afternoons were spent smoking, first behind the toilets, then down at the pub. His association with me kindled an interest in walking that built up to a steady glow and then a consuming blaze. Neither his parents nor his brothers could ever fathom his new enthusiasm for walking—and to this day, his family suspect me of having perverted their boy.

Recently, I unearthed a travel diary given to me by my parents for our first trip overseas as a couple. John wanted to go to the Greek Islands (he was still in his tinder stage and thought holidays were something you spent on a beach) but I persuaded him to visit the country of my birth. I assiduously filled in the various pages of the book, including 'Postcards Sent' and 'Gifts Purchased'. The first entry under 'Hotels Stopped At' is the Tavistock Hotel in London (here I note that two waiters had a punch-up during breakfast), but very soon we're drawn to smaller settlements (the Greyhound Inn in the village of Sydling St Nicholas had a dead mouse under the bath). Then, according to the journal, we're off on foot, with a day-walk to see the nearby Giant of Cerne Abbas, the surprisingly endowed male figure carved into the chalky Dorset hillside. The rest of the diary describes town visits interspersed with days spent walking in the country.

On the next big trip, there were fewer cities and we walked for a few days in sequence, leaving luggage at a railway station. The trip after that, after my first visit to the frenzied book fair that takes place annually in Frankfurt, we added a ten-day 'independent' walk, with luggage carried and accommodation organised for us. I wondered briefly whether ten days might not be a little too long, but by day three we were both hooked and on day eleven my body wanted to keep on walking. We quickly realised that there was no need to subscribe to a packaged walk: for the next post–book fair trip we shamelessly pored over the brochures of walking companies to choose a good destination, and off we went, by ourselves. And as soon as possible, we made walking a source of income—although this is really a thin excuse to maximise our walking excursions, which now occupy almost all our holidays. We are officially 'travel writers', which is pretty much akin to testers of trail footgear or plant collectors.

You may wish to conjure up your own excuse to keep non-walking interlocutors satisfied, but it's not essential. There are a growing number of sensible people out there who are choosing to walk simply for pleasure. Certainly, those who've challenged themselves on a long, well-chosen hike understand fully the lure of the next walk.

If you have yet to undertake such a journey, waste no further time. Read as much or as little of this book as you think necessary and get on your way.

2. *Spoilt for choice*

Your choice of how you tackle a long walk will be determined by your preferred comfort level, your physical capabilities, and to a large degree by where you wish to walk. No one method is superior to another, so those dedicated backpacking campers out there can wipe that smug look off their faces. However, if you have the flexibility to switch from mode to mode, then you can walk just about anywhere.

SELF-SUFFICIENT CAMPING

Robert Louis Stevenson, a man plagued by ill-health from childhood and condemned to an early death, took a surprisingly upbeat view of sleeping rough:

> Give to me the life I love,
> Let the lave go by me,

Give the jolly heaven above
And the byway nigh me.
Bed in a bush with stars to see,
Bread I dip in the river—
There's the life for a man like me,
There's the life for ever.
(FROM 'THE VAGABOND')

It is the romantic ideal: stopping wherever you feel tired, making a simple meal from the contents of your pack, and sleeping under the stars or at least with very little between you and them. In reality, you must choose your campsite carefully, eat a compromise of a meal, and sleep under cover in case of rain, frost or insects. Nonetheless, backpacking—carrying everything needed to sustain you and camping along the way—gives the walker great freedom and can bring many pleasures.

It also brings a lot of gear, though thankfully this has grown lighter over the years. Once you've covered the expense of the equipment, it is certainly the cheapest way to walk. Being self-sufficient allows you to walk in more remote areas, away from settlement of any kind. You do need water, though, and it's not possible to carry food for much more than five days. If you can't restock supplies as you pass through settlements, you may be able to arrange food drops. These days, many countries restrict where or how you can camp. Wild camping may be regulated in national parks to protect fragile landscapes, so check ahead before you pack the tent.

Theoretically, I understand the attractions of a night *en plein air*, and from time to time I submit myself to camping, but it's not my natural element. The nights are very long, the temperature is often cruel and the ground in too close contact with my hips. If I am persuaded to pitch a tent, it's usually as a base for remote day-walks. I actively avoid the need to carry tent, sleeping bag, mat and cooking utensils each day, as the extra burden reduces my enjoyment of a good walk. John likes to imply that I'm the only impediment to him taking on the role of self-sufficient bushman, but he enjoys a degree of ease as much as I.

HUT TO HUT

Our preference is for a light burden that allows us to walk independently from bed to bed. On popular long walks, we are often alone in carrying all our own gear, but when your full pack only weighs twelve kilos this is no great hardship. When walking in New Zealand, we have the added weight of food, fuel and stove, but all our rambles in Europe are devised so we can find beds and sustenance along the way. These may be village-to-village walks staying in inns; they can be refuge to refuge, farm to farm or a mixture of each. Our own itineraries in European mountains usually include nights in upper-valley villages as well as mountain refuges, since being well fed and well rested is conducive to walking greater distances. Walking hut to hut or village to village does require extra work at the planning stage: it takes time to discover obscure forms of accommodation in depopulated areas. This mode of walking also dictates to an extent where we walk, but we have yet to run out of either enthusiasm or destinations.

ASSISTED WALKING

Between the rigours of self-sufficiency and the convenience of joining a group trek lie several other alternatives.

Baggage transfer

Using this service you head off on foot with a day pack and someone else drives the balance of your gear to your night's destination. You might have a non-walking friend who would be prepared to do this for you, meeting up each evening but doing their own thing during the day. Along some long-distance footpaths in Britain, certain accommodation providers will transport your bags to your next overnight stop. We found this a wonderful option when walking the Ridgeway with my eighty-year-old father. Depending on how he was coping, we would decide how far to walk the next day, then book a pub or B&B accordingly so that our host had an address to deliver the bags.

On more popular British routes, such as Scotland's West Highland Way and England's Coast-to-Coast, commercial operators can transport your luggage along the entire route and also book accommodation for you. They have elaborate websites where you specify how far you wish to walk and how much money you wish to spend on a bed. Their charges are very reasonable, but there is a lack of flexibility once you've made those decisions. I've noticed that this option does encourage people to overpack; we met one woman who had packed six pairs of shoes because she wasn't sure which would be most comfortable. Judging by her blisters, none of them were.

Self-guided packages

There's further assistance but even less flexibility if you commit to a self-guided package. The additional help comes in the form of detailed walk notes and maps for a route that may be less well known, along with half-board accommodation (that is, with breakfasts and dinners) and baggage transfer. Human transfers between a city and the start or end of the walk may also be included. We once made use of a package arranged by an entrepreneurial German tourist office in the Black Forest and were rewarded with an obscure but pleasing circular route with a selection of colourful inns or *gasthofs* that we wouldn't have otherwise discovered. Numerous businesses offer such packages in a variety of countries, especially in Europe, and a few are listed at the back of this book.

This type of package allows you to select your own departure date (within a specified walking season) and to keep your own company. Such affairs are more expensive than if you booked the same accommodation yourself, but much of the fiddly work has been done for you.

Pack animals

Hannibal enjoyed his independence but he still made use of pack animals to help carry the load when he took elephants over the Col de la Seigne below Mont Blanc in 219 BC. Well, all right, maybe the elephants were just for show. There are, after all, other animals that are more sure-footed and docile.

Pack animals are only necessary if you plan to camp and wish to carry enough food for an extended walk. Once Robert

Louis Stevenson had assembled his gentleman-goes-to-the-hills paraphernalia (which included an egg-beater), the only way of transporting it over the Cévennes in France was via a beast of burden, namely a donkey called Modestine. You'll be pleased to hear that, for a price, you can replicate his journey *avec* donkey. However, as Stevenson discovered, a donkey (or its relative the mule) can be uncooperative, so you may decide to seek professional help in the form of a mule-driver. In poorer countries where beasts of burden are valuable livestock, you'll probably find that hiring a mule-driver is compulsory. In such cases, you may need to provide the mule-driver with food and tent space, and perhaps to pay them for their return trip. Getting complicated, isn't it?

Llamas make picturesque pack animals, but they can't carry as much as donkeys—and they spit. So do camels. I'm not sure about yaks.

Guides and porters

On some treks, such as Peru's Inca Trail, Borneo's Gunung Kinabalu, or the ascent of Mount Kilimanjaro, you have no choice other than to walk with local guides and porters. At high altitudes, where your physical abilities will be compromised, you are more likely to need this level of assistance. These services can usually be acquired from the nearest regional centre—for example, Kathmandu in the Himalaya, or Cusco in Peru. When you hire guides, they usually take on the responsibilities of hiring porters, translating the local language for you and navigating the route, but you should negotiate all details of the trek in advance. Don't assume that they will give you a running commentary on landscapes and culture as you go, but do ask plenty of questions along the way.

FULLY SERVICED

If you are new to journeying by foot, desire the company of others or wish to walk in an area where the practicalities are complex, you might turn to the commercial trek operator. Increasing numbers of companies are offering guided or 'escorted' walking excursions. When choosing one, heed the recommendations of friends or, failing this, feature articles written by familiar travel writers. When a company offers walks in an array of countries, check who will be operating the trek that interests you; sometimes it will be run by a local, allied business. This may have minor consequences—a talkative but monolingual friend found she was the only non-French speaker on a trek in France that she'd booked through an English company. In some countries, walks must be arranged with registered local companies, but it's good to know who these are in advance.

Relying on a professional guide can substitute for a degree of outdoor experience, but this shouldn't mean you abrogate all personal responsibilities. Pay close attention to how a trek has been graded, and don't sign up for something beyond your physical capabilities or mental stamina. Some commercial trekking operators require a medical certificate from your doctor, but it's still *your* responsibility to choose a suitable hike. Make sure you are comfortable with the walking distances planned for each day, and with the duration of the walk. If you prefer a full day's walk, be wary of itineraries where you spend a large part of your holiday being shuttled between short strolls. The programs for different companies tend to have a distinct pitch that becomes clear when you peruse their brochures; some simply include a few half-day walks on what is otherwise a conventional tour of a country or region. Don't join an organised trek if you don't like taking instructions—and also remember that, as part of a group, you will need to behave in a way that benefits the party as a whole. As the statesman Edmund Burke noted centuries ago, 'Society is indeed a contract.' You might want to check how large a society yours will be.

There are lots of benefits to be gained from a guided walk, particularly in less developed countries. Language gaps are bridged, logistics and bureaucratic matters handled. Baggage is usually transported by vehicle, local porters or their animals. Staff may also walk on ahead to set up camp and prepare a meal for you. While this certainly alleviates many of the privations of camping, it is still essentially camping: sleeping on the ground with limited protection from potentially harsh weather. Walkers aren't the only ones to gain from the equation—the employment of local people provides a great economic boost at a grassroots level. Well-planned treks aren't an unexpected drag on limited local supplies of food and fuel; the leaders usually carry tinned and dried foods with them and supplement these with fresh vegetables as they pass through villages that are prepared for their custom. Organised treks should also carry their own fuel so that timber isn't required for cooking food.

The growth in this approach to travel opens up lots of possibilities for walking around the world. It can also extend your walking life. My parents' adventures became more exotic as they aged: they joined commercial treks to the Himalaya in their sixties and to Patagonia and Borneo in their seventies. I hope to follow in their footsteps.

FINDING YOUR COMFORT LEVEL

These, then, are the options. Those who have, up to now, only ventured out on day-walks might benefit from assistance on their first long walk. In 'tamer' walking areas, you can opt for independence, arrange for your baggage to be transferred or join an escorted walk. In more remote or wild places, your choices will probably be confined to complete self-sufficiency, arranging guides and support on arrival, or fully guided commercial trekking. Your budget, how much you care to rough it and how much you're prepared to carry will determine to a large degree where you can walk.

Being self-sufficient for food and shelter gives you the freedom to attempt long trails in North America or Australia. For those who wish to walk independently but not sleep outdoors, the walking world is a slightly smaller oyster. Europe offers almost every kind of landscape complete with hostelries where someone will even cook you a hearty meal. Simple accommodation is appearing along popular trekking routes in other parts of the world, but you will need to research your options before you go.

Another consideration that affects personal comfort is climate—and, more particularly, temperature. You might wish for soaring temperatures on a beach holiday, but it won't do for hiking up hills. My Scottish genesis has resulted in a particularly poor thermostat for self-regulating body temperature in warm conditions: I just don't sweat enough. Instead I overheat, turn the colour of a blood orange and suffer the unpleasant sensation that my brain is boiling. On the other hand, I can endure surprisingly low temperatures as long as I'm moving and know that I can keep warm when I stop. For me, a comfortable temperature range for walking is from –5 to 20°C, and I, like most, prefer a dry heat to high humidity. This makes walking in subtropical climes far less appealing to me. If you enjoy walking in warmer conditions your set of possible walking destinations will be broader, or at least different.

Altitude also affects some people more than others, and unfortunately this can't be predicted on the basis of age or fitness. Another variable that will affect some walkers is a fear of exposure. Sufferers of vertigo would do well to stay clear of routes along sea cliffs or the 'iron ways' that run along the elevated ledges of the Italian Dolomites. If you merely have a mild form of risk aversion, as many city-dwellers do, summon the courage to be adventurous. I'm not advocating foolhardiness—people can die on holiday because they take physical risks that they would never dream of normally—but if you actively challenge yourself, your walk will be that much more memorable.

Foremost, you need to take into account the limitations of your fitness: how much up hill and down dale is too much? If you desire level walking, you could consider paths where you're assured of a gentle gradient: canal towpaths or railway lines that have been reassigned as walking and cycling paths. Hilly or mountainous countryside is not, however, the sole preserve of the ultra-fit: walking paths often thread a route between the peaks, either along the valley floors or contouring the flanks. Find a destination that challenges but does not kill you, and make sensible use of any assistance on offer.

3. *Finding your stride*

. . . .

'Walking is really progressing in a straight line . . . using the hips, knees, ankles and toes as flexibly as possible, so that at each step the body is pushed forward by the toes and the head moves forward in a smooth line.' So wrote Editha Hearn back in 1967 in *You Are as Young as Your Spine*. Editha also advised that women are much safer wearing an elastic girdle. They don't call people Editha any more.

Of course, there are different modes of walking: there's pottering about the garden, ducking down to the local shop for more milk, or even trudging home when you've missed the bus. And then there's striding out to the whole stretch of your limbs, harnessing the spring in your toes while rediscovering the capacity of your lungs. When you are in full swing, your movement is instinctive and everything seems balanced and true.

THE MECHANICS OF WALKING

The main difference between hiking and plebeian walking is that you'll probably be carrying something on your back. At least, that's where it should be: carrying water bottles or cameras in your hands isn't viable on a long walk. (We'll come back to the topic of bearing a load in Chapter 8.) While walking, simply keep as upright as you can and establish your own natural stride. That's it. For those who want further guidance, here are some tips for walking over varying terrain.

Ascents

Some people like the *concept* of walking, but not the actuality of ups and downs. These are, however, unavoidable on a long walk and shouldn't be viewed as inherently unpleasant. Adam Nicolson, an English enthusiast writing an article on an alpine crossing, goes so far as to embrace ascents:

> As you climb, a strange process begins to overtake both mind and body. It may be something to do with the obviousness of the enterprise—from one valley over a mountain to the next—and something about the simple, one-foot-in-front-of-the-other sweat of it, but the sensation is of growing purity, of uninvolved, hard purity.

All right, you want some practical advice. On a gradient, take shorter steps. On a steep uphill, you might prefer to zigzag: it will take longer but leave you less exhausted. Some hikers recommend the 'rest step' on a steep climb: pausing for a second after planting the forward foot. I suspect I've been using this technique without realising it, although I call it the 'feeling knackered step'. If a steep slope has a soft, loose surface, climb it with your feet placed sideways. Using a pair of trekking poles to pull your body up a hill can make an ascent less demanding on the legs, while making use of arm muscles you may not have realised existed.

There are different psychological approaches to ascending a long, continuous slope. John prefers the dogged one, making his feet labour on until the top is achieved; I stop often and pretend to enjoy the scenery while I muster the will to continue. Either way, be wary of 'false peaks', as setting your target on what turns out to be simply a bulge on the spur you are climbing can be very demoralising. I can make one promise: ascending becomes easier after the first couple of days, though descending may not.

Descents

Most walkers find descents are harder work than equivalent ascents, partly because they're already weary from achieving the latter. Descending makes quite different demands on your leg muscles, and a long descent can certainly be hard on the muscles in the front of the thighs and also on the knee joints. Allow your knees to bend with each step so that the legs aren't jarred on impact. If the track is broad, zigzagging across it may help. Adjustable poles are a great boon on a long descent, particularly if the ground surface is loose; I'll harp on about them a lot more in Chapter 8.

Steep bits

Occasionally, you might find yourself having to use all four limbs to *scramble*—sort of like rock climbing without the serious gear.

You don't need to be among mountains to scramble: coastal gullies, river beds and escarpments often demand a bit of it. Try to have three points of contact at all times: for example, two handholds and one foot secure while the other foot moves. Steep ascent is almost always easier than descent, so don't go blithely scrambling up a rocky pinnacle only to find yourself stranded. When descending with a heavy pack, avoid jumping down as the weight can unbalance you and your landing will be more jarring on the joints and spine than usual.

Scree

Isn't it a delightful word? Scree is the collection of loose rock fragments on a mountain slope, usually found at the base of a rock face or in the moraine of a retreating glacier, and I suspect the name derives from the sound your boot makes as you try to gain some purchase on it. The ground slides away with each step, making a scree slope very tiring to ascend. Climb sideways, keeping your weight over your feet and kicking side-steps in it. When descending a scree slope, avoid the temptation to run—'scree-skiing', as Mark Twain did down Vesuvius—as this will degrade the slope and can be dangerous. Dig your heels in firmly but avoid leaning back. Poles are again invaluable on this terrain.

Talus or boulders

Larger rocks and small boulders in mountainous terrain are called talus. At lower levels, river beds may offer a similar surface. In both cases, never assume a rock is stable. That doesn't mean you have to test out each one before tentatively putting down your weight: if you have a good sense of balance, your best mode of walking might be rock-hopping, which is more akin to dancing than walking. Take short steps and develop a momentum as you move from rock to rock so that, if one does shift, your weight is already being transferred to the next. When your route crosses a boulder field, note the direction you must take before you start, as you'll need to concentrate on your footing while you're moving.

Sand

Those pictures of lovers strolling on a beach without a care in the world are a tad misleading: walking down a long beach can be surprisingly tiring on the muscles in the feet and calves. It's decidedly easier to walk along a beach when the tide is dropping and the sand is still wet. Dry sand behaves in the same way as scree, making ascending sandy slopes quite tiring. Take care not to erode sand dunes by running down them, and avoid getting sand in your shoes, which may cause blisters.

Clay

Clay baked in the sun or frozen solid can be very hard on the feet and, if it's rutted by bike wheels or vehicles, a risk to your ankles. Waterlogged clay is extremely slippery. Ploughed clay can be very tacky and accumulate in large gobbets on your boots. Scrape it off every now and then or you'll tire from the extra weight. Much of the Ridgeway, a prehistoric trading route over England's North Wessex Downs and the Chilterns, is white clay: goodness knows how the Neanderthals coped.

Greasy rock

Rock that is covered with moss or mud, or worn smooth (as limestone or glacier-scraped granite often is) and made wet, can be extremely slippery. River beds, where the rocks remain damp from changing water levels, offer lots of ankle-twisting opportunities. Place your feet carefully, onto level rocks rather than angled ones, and have a handhold if possible. If in doubt, step between rocks rather than on them.

Wood

Wet wood can be unbelievably slippery. All my worst tumbles have been on wood, including tree roots, an erosion barrier and, embarrassingly, simple wooden steps. Take care too when putting your weight on wood that may have rotted.

Road

An asphalt road is not a particularly tricky surface, but a long road-walk is a sure engenderer of blisters and sore feet. If there's a softer verge, walk on that occasionally. English historian (and serious distance walker) G.M. Trevelyan wrote that 'the road is invaluable for pace and swing' but that 'twenty-five or thirty miles of moor and mountain, of wood and field-path, is better in every way than five-and-thirty, or even forty, hammered out on the road'. And Trevelyan didn't even have to worry about many motor cars. Walk facing oncoming traffic so you have a chance to step aside if necessary.

Snow

No special equipment is needed to cross a light covering of soft snow. On a slope, kick your toes in if you are ascending and your heels if you are descending, but keep your weight over your feet in both cases. If the snow is hard or icy (as it can be in early spring when late-lying snow is subjected to thaws and freezes) it can be very slippery, and you might need to kick the side of your boot into the path to get a better hold. We have been known to glissade down a soft, deep, snowy slope by sitting down and sliding. It's a bit silly, as you're at risk of hitting a sharp rock or of being unable to stop the descent, so we always let a friend go first.

If you're planning to walk over steep or permanent snowfields—glaciers—you should carry crampons and a lightweight ice axe. Crampons are metal attachments for your boots that have prongs for gripping snow or ice. You can't leave them on all day or they'll soon be blunted by rocks, so you should get deft at attaching and removing them in the cold. An ice axe can be used like a walking stick by holding the head, but it can also be employed to cut steps. Most importantly, you can use it to stop yourself from sliding uncontrollably down a slope with the technique of self-arrest by lying face down with the axe head under your armpit and using the pick end as a brake. (This technique should obviously be practised before you need to use it.) If the mere idea terrifies you, simply restrict your high mountain walking to summer and stay well away from crevassed glaciers.

Water

A route can be icy early in the morning and even well into the day if it lies in shade. When rock is covered in ice, it is downright dangerous and you should take care to have a handhold or to step in the cracks between rocks. I was once bemused by a party of French walkers in the Pyrenees who greeted us with calls of '*Glace!*' Strange, I thought, that there should be a kiosk selling ice cream at such altitude. Then we stumbled down the frozen stream that followed the course of the path.

More likely, you'll encounter water in its unfrozen state, as streams or rivers. This is quite a major issue as running water can be extremely powerful, so I've covered river crossings in Chapter 12, 'Obstacles and aids'.

Bog

This could be peat bog, cow-pasture bog or bog-standard bog: any way it's a bugger. If your path crosses waterlogged ground, grit your teeth and be prepared to get wet feet. A pair of gaiters limits the amount of ooze getting in the top of your boots, and you can use trekking poles for stability and to test the ground ahead if it's really deep. Much of the lauded Overland Track in highland Tasmania crosses terrain prone to waterlogging, so solid boardwalks have been built to safeguard the fragile vegetation. If you detour off the main track to ascend nearby peaks, however, you can find yourself stepping into and hauling out of groin-deep, boggy trenches: extremely tiring work that slows progress considerably. Don't let me put you off, though; the views gained make every squelch worthwhile.

Whenever walking and whatever the terrain, the trick is to be alert to the nature of the ground you're covering and to place your feet carefully, opting for dry, durable surfaces where possible.

PAUSING

There is some disagreement about taking rests. Handbook author H.D. Westacott advises that the secret of walking long distances

> is not so much walking fast as to keep going with a minimum of stops . . . Train yourself to walk for three or four hours at a stretch without stops except perhaps for two or three minutes at the summit of a stiff climb. When you do stop for a meal and rest, choose a comfortable spot out of the wind, take off your boots and rucksack and after eating and drinking lie flat on your back for fifteen minutes and relax completely.

Oh, the stoicism of the British, eh? I have more empathy with his American counterpart John Hart, who explains:

> Physiologically, several short rests are better than one long one. As your muscles work, they build up a waste called lactic acid. When you rest, you can get rid of about thirty percent of this waste in five to seven minutes. But fifteen more minutes of rest will eliminate only another five percent.

Sod the percentages: if I want a rest, I'll take one.

Sometimes you'll reach a spot that dictates a stop: a grassy lakeside, the dramatic edge of an escarpment or the bank of a rippling stream. Other times, something else will necessitate a stop: hunger, a sighting of an animal, a stone in your boot. If your body needs a rest, lean back against a tree or your pack and stretch your legs out in front; they'll thank you for a little elevation. At the risk of sounding like your mother, I also recommend that you don a jacket to make sure you don't get chilled.

LOW-IMPACT WALKING

The impact of hiking on the environment is, admittedly, nothing compared with the effects of mining, logging, damming or simply of habitation. Yet we choose to walk through certain areas because of their near-pristine condition and we have every reason to preserve it that way for others to enjoy.

Whenever possible, walk on durable surfaces such as rock and sand. Avoid stepping on vegetation, especially in fragile environments such as tundra or desert where plants grow very slowly. If you're walking on a path, do just that. Don't create a shortcut to avoid the corner of a trail zigzagging a slope; this can cause erosion. Even if such shortcuts are already there, stick to the main path. If a path is prone to waterlogging, avoid the temptation to walk on drier ground alongside, as this will only broaden the boggy section. Keep the path narrow by walking in single file wherever suitable. Take care not to create secondary paths, especially in areas where snow patches are thawing and the ground below is moist and fragile. Lesson over.

SPEED AND DISTANCE

In 1066, by unfortunate coincidence, England was invaded almost simultaneously by the Norwegians and the Normans. England's king, Harold Godwinson, managed to hotfoot it north from London to York with 7000 men—covering 185 miles in seven days and averaging 26.4 miles (or 42.5 kilometres) a day—and took the pesky Norwegians by surprise, soundly defeating them at the torrid Battle of Stamford Bridge. Pretty impressive, eh? He then had to turn his troops around and march them 241 miles south through London and on to Hastings, where the result wasn't quite so good for Harold.

The obvious moral here is that you should know your limitations when walking long distances (and carrying heavy chain mail). Robert Louis Stevenson counsels against 'overwalking' and considers someone who walks too far and too fast to be intemperate: 'It is the fate of such a one to take twice as much trouble as is needed to obtain happiness, and miss the happiness in the end; he is the man of the proverb, in short, who goes further and fares worse.' Stevenson probably didn't have Harold specifically in mind, but you couldn't fare a lot worse than getting an arrow in your eye.

Past generations undoubtedly walked further and faster than we do today. I read somewhere that one afternoon poet William Wordsworth and his sister Dorothy walked seventeen miles over a mountain road in little more than four hours. That's a cracking pace of more than 6.5 kilometres an hour, and she had to do it in a long skirt. Nineteenth-century mountaineers covered great distances on foot: Edward Whymper, who conquered the Matterhorn, spoke of one fellow adventurer who regularly covered forty miles a day as being a reasonably good walker.

Another mountaineer, the Reverend Charles Hudson, is said to have averaged fifty miles a day on foot.

It's not a race, so there's no reason you would want to emulate such feats. However, it is important to be able to estimate how long a walk will take, particularly if daylight hours are short or if you have a transport connection to catch. In 1892 yet another walker-climber, William Naismith from Scotland, devised a formula for estimating the time required to walk a distance. Using Naismith's formula, you should allow one hour for every three miles (almost five kilometres) of distance and add a half-hour for every 1000 feet (300 metres or so) of ascent. To this I would add that you should allow extra time for:

- meal stops
- bad weather (including headwinds)
- difficult terrain
- route-finding problems
- rest breaks on a long day's walk
- walking in a group
- heavy packs.

A heavy pack, for example, can drop the average speed to three kilometres per hour on level ground. Of course, some elements of a walk can't be predicted. In Australia, it's easy to get 'bushwhacked' when thick vegetation has reclaimed your track and you have to push through thickets, something a map won't tell you in advance. With experience, you'll get a clearer idea of the effect of factors such as terrain on walking time, but if you are estimating it afresh, you should allow plenty of extra time and daylight.

You also need to establish your own pace and to discover the distance with which you are comfortable. I'm happy walking thirty kilometres a day over easy ground but some would think this unnecessarily arduous. A friend who is far more energetic says she'd be physically incapable of walking such distances. In mountainous terrain, we more often average fifteen kilometres a day. It may not sound like much, but if that includes gaining a kilometre in ascent (and usually a similar descent) we feel satisfied that we've had a good day out.

Most often, you'll have reference to a guide book or walk notes that indicate a distance, grade and walking time for each day's journey. Distance is a straightforward matter, but the grading will often be more informative. It should take into account the amount of ascent and descent (which some books will also advise separately) and the roughness of the trail. It must also assume good weather conditions. Any times specified will only be someone's estimate and you should check how these have been calculated; if they are actual walking times and haven't allowed time for food breaks, toilet stops and scenery gazing, then you will need to add a large dollop of time. You'll also need to gauge their standards: are they pitching at casual walkers with grandmothers in tow, or at those taut young men you see running up mountains in silken boxer shorts? You may not get a good handle on a guide book's grading and times until you've walked a couple of its routes yourself.

GETTING UP TO SPEED

These days, most of us lead sedentary lives: we drive or catch transport to work, where we sit in front of a screen with only the occasional stroll to the coffee machine for exercise. Back home we sit in front of the television or relax with the newspaper. It would be foolish to attempt a long walk from a standing (or seated) start, but how much preparation is necessary depends on your level of fitness. As long as you're reasonably fit, the only training you'll probably need is a bit of walking. Just how much of a bit depends on how strenuous a walk you are planning.

Before departing, undertake a couple of day-walks at least the same length as you plan to walk each day on your excursion. Wear the boots or shoes you plan to take. This allows you either to 'break in' new boots or to discover any flaws that have developed in an old pair. My brother-in-law recently walked Tasmania's Overland Track in seldom-used boots that, by day two, had to be taped onto him each morning and cut off him each evening. You should also prepare for carrying the pack weight. This can be achieved by carrying heavy items in a day-pack—at lunch on a preparatory walk, our friend Pete pulled from his pack two hefty volumes of the Sydney telephone directory and asked if we wanted to call anyone—but it is also wise to get used to the backpack you will be taking, in case you want to make any adjustments before you leave.

For any distance walking, day after day, you will need stamina. You need to be physically prepared and the fitter you are at the start, the more you can relax and enjoy the scenery. But being physically capable of the task isn't sufficient; you also require mental stamina. You need to be prepared for bad weather, physical discomfort and even boredom. I can't stress this enough. We met a fellow from Birmingham midway along the Coast-to-Coast walk that crosses northern England. It was his first long walk and, despite being quite fit in body, he appeared to be doing it extremely tough. He was walking solo and for some people that exacerbates the trials of a long walk. Little in his demeanour suggested he was enjoying the journey, there was only grim determination. He most likely achieved his goal but I doubt very much he would undertake such an enterprise again for pleasure.

And it is meant to be pleasurable. The reasons for improving your walking techniques are (a) to make the pastime more enjoyable and (b) to reduce the risk of injury, which contributes further to (a). Once you know what speed and distances best suit you, you're in a much better position to plan a walking holiday.

Next, there's the matter of choosing a backdrop for your adventure.

4. Setting the scene

......

Every landscape is different, shaped over time by a unique combination of geology and climate, and affected to varying degrees by *Homo sapiens*. Humans have always had a tendency to treat wilderness as a special category. Once it was feared for being inhospitable or dismissed as barren and then, following the Romantics, elevated as sublime. In this later scheme, some physical features—mountains, lofty waterfalls, ancient forests—are valued above swamps, moors and grasslands. Yet Ansel Adams, who famously photographed Yosemite Valley, understood that 'in the last analysis, Half Dome is just a piece of rock' and that it is our own 'deep personal distillation of spirit and concept' that elevates it.

Not only are all landscapes inherently equal, the way we value pristine wilds over cultivated land is dubious: aren't humans, after all, part of nature? In this egalitarian approach, landscapes just lie at different positions along the culture–wilderness spectrum that stretches from city, via town, through cultivated ground, to land less clearly marked by human activity. All scenery can hold interest for the thoughtful walker (although, admittedly, swamps can prove hard to love), but any clear preference for one end of the spectrum over the other may help you select a destination.

THE MYSTERY OF MOUNTAINS

Most of us find it very difficult to resist the charms of mountains, presumably because they force us to acknowledge our limitations and put our piddling concerns in perspective. British artist and critic John Ruskin summed it up nicely when he proclaimed that 'mountains are the beginning and the end of all natural scenery'. There's a whole vocabulary set aside for mountainscapes, much of it drawn from the French tongue: *cirque*, *arête*, *aiguille* and *massif*.

You don't need to be a thrill-seeking climber to enjoy mountain views. As long as you're fit, with a little extra effort you can leave the valley floor and walk up to a pass (or *col*) allowing you to cross from one valley to the next and gain new vistas. You need not even scale peaks for a sense of achievement: walking a circuit of a mountain has a long tradition as a form of religious pilgrimage. Mount Kailash, in southern Tibet, is circled by both Hindu and Buddhist pilgrims on a gruelling trek. There is inevitably a degree of effort involved—the Tour (or circuit) of Mont Blanc demands at least 8000 metres of ascent and descent to cross over passes—but encircling such a massif is a unique way of appreciating its complexity of form.

Not all mountains are the same: most are formed along the convergence of tectonic plates, but then other factors—such as folding, volcanic activity or glaciation—come into play. New Zealand's islands were shaped by different processes: the North is volcanic, the South uplifted and glaciated. In Western Europe, the volcanic Massif Central is a stone's throw from the folded mountains of the Alps which in turn are a mere spit away from the uplifted marine reef that formed the rock obelisks of the Dolomites. Luckily the world has buckled and erupted nicely in many places and only Holland is flat as a pancake. There are walking paths among the High Tatras on the border of Poland and Slovakia, in Yugoslavia's Montenegro, among the Pindos of Greece and in the Taurus Mountains in southern Turkey. And that's just in Europe. Depending on latitude and climate, you can find mountains that are snow-capped or arid, with slopes that are jungle, ancient forest, or pasture sprinkled with wildflowers.

Freestanding volcanoes, formed over hot spots, can be very dramatic and are more easily encircled than mountains in a massif. If you enjoy the thrill of live volcanoes, consider Etna in Sicily, Tongariro in New Zealand, and plenty of spluttering ones in Hawaii and Iceland. On the negative side, young volcanic landscapes can be barren, desolate and hot underfoot. Smoothly graded, extinct or long-dormant volcanoes offer the highest peaks that non-mountaineers can summit: Mount Kenya at 4985 metres, and Kilimanjaro another thousand metres higher. Just take your time ascending: the consequences of not acclimatising can be dire.

Those who have a penchant for glaciers (my hand is up) had better hurry before they all melt away. Glaciers have almost disappeared off Mount Kilimanjaro. We've stayed in European refuges where old photographs hanging on the wall can be compared with the view out the window for a punchy lesson on global warming. The Alps, Andes, Rockies and Himalaya still reward walkers with views of 'permanent' (as opposed to seasonal) glaciers. In New Zealand, Patagonia and Alaska, walkers can get up close to the snout of a glacier without the trouble of ascending to high altitudes. Standing by the torrent of meltwater emerging from under a wall of ice is an astounding experience.

UNTAMED SCENERY

Mountains aren't the only topography to have repulsed human habitation. Anywhere the soil is thin or waterlogged is likely to be sparsely populated and exhibit a certain grandeur. Desert is one extreme that is not conducive to walking for extended periods, although there are commercial hikes (with camels) that provide a flavour of the Australian desert. Vast moorland has a similar effect; the monotony of it makes the walker turn inward for diversion. Still, a few days on the North Yorkshire Moors can be highly rewarding, with a surprising variety of birdlife to enjoy. Limestone pavements have a different fascination, with their clints and grikes (more wonderful landscape terms!), but can be tricky underfoot.

Anywhere that the rocky skeleton of the land is exposed is worth close inspection. Particularly spectacular and diverting to the eye are steep-sided canyons and gorges. There is a whole region in America's west called the Canyonlands that includes the famous Grand Canyon and the mighty Zion National Park. Elsewhere, the various gorges in southern France, Jordan, Namibia or the Kakadu of northern Australia all invite the walker to pass through in awe. Strange rock formations are always a worthy destination: the red hoodoos of Bryce Canyon in Utah or the bizarre white pillars and cones of Cappadocia in Turkey make a dramatic backdrop for a walk.

WATERSIDE

Essayist Joseph Addison was on to something when he wrote, in 1712, 'there is nothing that more enlivens a prospect than rivers, jetteaus, or falls of water, where the scene is perpetually shifting, and entertaining the sight every moment with something that is new'. As well as quenching a walker's thirst, a good river or waterfall engages the imagination. One of the greatest delights is seeing a river grow: encountering a spring trickling out of a hillside, and following it down over a number of days as it cascades off the high country and gathers momentum to become a serious river like the French Loire or the River Dee of my birthplace. A waterway can seem like an old friend when you cross it repeatedly (or perhaps an old adversary if there's no bridge).

Gentle river valleys are often the repository of fertile soil, and there's plenty of pleasant walking in such broad river valleys as those of the Dordogne in France or the Wye in Wales, or in steep-sided valleys such as New Zealand's Hollyford.

Some, like Irish poet W.B. Yeats, are drawn to water that pools:

I will arise and go now, for always night and day
I hear lake water lapping with low sounds by the shore;
While I stand on the roadway, or on the pavements grey,
I hear it in the deep heart's core.

(FROM 'THE LAKE ISLE OF INNISFREE')

Don't those lines make you want to rise and go with him to Lough Gill in County Sligo? Years earlier, across the Atlantic, Henry David Thoreau had found inspiration (and plenty of good walking) by the banks of tiny Walden Pond in Massachusetts. An intimate pool suited the reclusive Thoreau; for expansive personalities, there is more grandeur to be found in larger bodies of water, particularly in those regions carved out by departed glaciers. The English Lakes bear quaint names such as Crummock Water or Buttermere that play down their dramatic origins and sound instead like an old-fashioned remedy for dyspepsia. In the Canadian Rockies, names such as Emerald Lake and Moraine Lake are decidedly more informative. For your exotic *lago*, you could head to Bariloche in Argentina, or to Lombardy in Italy's north. For the really exotic, you could make your way to Kyrgyzstan's 'Lakes of the Sky'. In lake districts, you can choose to promenade on relatively level ground around large, scenic sheets of water, or you can spend days clambering up the surrounding hillsides to glittering tarns perched in hanging valleys high above.

And then there's coastal walking, visiting secluded coves and encountering rugged sea cliffs and towering stacks isolated by wild seas and home to nesting seabirds. For those who imagine coastal walking to be a doddle, keep in mind that between every pair of beaches there's inevitably a headland to be negotiated. Exposed sections can be so windy as to render conversation pointless. We have enjoyed walking stretches of the coast of Brittany, Liguria, south-west England, south-east Australia and New Zealand; our next destination is the shores of southern Turkey to walk part of the Lycian Way. There are plenty of beaches and crinkly bits out there. You might consider the Algarve in Portugal, Croatia's Dalmatian coast, or the Otter Trail in South Africa.

WILDWOODS

Across cultures, the tree—and by extension woodland—is a potent symbol of the life force. At times when boughs creak overhead, leaves rustle and light plays a complex dance, a wood can appear to have a life apart. Poet Walt Whitman certainly found them stimulating: 'Why are there trees I never walk under but large and melodious thoughts descend upon me?' More prosaically, they also provide the walker with shade and shelter from light rainfall.

Forests of plantation evergreens can be dull and monotonous, particularly those that allow little light to reach the ground and nourish undergrowth. However, woodland doesn't have to be primeval and untouched to be fascinating; there is plenty of forest that has been managed for hundreds of years yet has an air of enchantment. The Black Forest or *Schwarzwald* is the base for Germany's oldest walking organisation, which since 1864 has maintained a network of footpaths through 'working' woods. Corsica's interior includes beautiful oak and chestnut woods replete with foraging pigs; apparently much of medieval England was like this, with people living and working in the woods.

There are so many types of treescape to explore. The vast Australian bush can prove surprisingly varied: there are more than 700 species of eucalyptus tree alone. New Zealand harbours strange trees and shrubs only slightly evolved from the ancient forests of Gondwanaland. For tropical rainforest or lush jungle, you might head to the canyons of Peru and Bolivia, to Sabah in Borneo or to the low-lying Cardamom Mountains in Cambodia. For something fragile and rare, take a walk in a mist forest where vegetation, frequently bathed in low cloud, grows into a miniature wonderland of small trees, epiphytic ferns, lichens and orchids. You can find these only at certain latitudes and elevations near the coast, for example in Ecuador and Borneo. Luckily for me, there is also a tiny patch of it on top of Lord Howe Island, off the eastern coast of Australia.

SIGNS OF LIFE

To many walkers, particularly those with a classical leaning, the ideal landscape is well ordered, with fields, vineyards, streams and woods all harmoniously placed. Despite my attraction to the needles and spires of mountains, an emerald-green pastoral scene pulls on a different subset of my heartstrings. Humankind generally lived in happy accord with the landscape—until someone foolishly invented concrete—and signs of that lighter way of living can be both enlightening and aesthetically pleasing.

Wayfarers get to appreciate this more than others. It is remarkable to encounter, in remote places, traces of early human activity: ancient stone circles, Celtic dolmens, grooves worn smooth in sandstone by Australian Aborigines sharpening their tools. A walk in the Dordogne region can take in a dozen sites of prehistoric significance, including delicately painted caves and troglodyte villages. In countries foreign to us, old land practices still in use can also please: in southern Spain we got a thrill each time we found an *era*, a stone threshing platform built at the edge of an escarpment so the breeze can blow away the chaff and leave the heavier grain. *Acequias*, ingenious irrigation systems built by the long-departed Moors, also spoke of human ingenuity in a harsh landscape. Throughout history, monasteries—both Western and Eastern—were sited in remote places so their inhabitants could avoid earthly distractions. Castles, in various states of ruin, make a stirring discovery for walkers in a frontier landscape.

There can be great romance in following an ancient route. Britain is crisscrossed by Roman roads that are in better condition than many built a decade ago by your local council. On the Nakasendo Way in Japan you can follow an unspoilt section of the seventh-century highway that once connected Kyoto to Tokyo. In Norway, you can take the medieval pilgrimage road from Oslo to Trondheim. In China, you can trek along sections of the astounding Great Wall. Likewise, the course of Hadrian's Wall can be traced as it snakes across northern England. Between high and low ground all over Europe, you can follow the route taken by herders and their animals up to summer pasture, in the annual transhumance that has taken place for centuries.

Rolling hills of permanent farmland also have much to offer (newborn lambs for one). The trend towards huge expanses of a single crop is not such a joy, but there are still plenty of regions where you'll pass fallow fields ablaze with poppies or buttercups. It's hard not to swoon over the patchwork fields of England's Yorkshire Dales, each pocket of green enclosed by dry-stone walls and dotted with a stone barn. A steep Asian or Peruvian hillside of perfectly cut terraces is likewise a true spectacle. A field full of purple lavender in Provence is a balm to the senses, but it's a sight granted only in the too-hot-for-me summer months.

Vineyards are a special category of cultivated land, holding the extra promise of a post-walk tasting. Also, where there's wine there's inevitably good food. Alsace, at the foot of the Vosges on the Franco-German border is an ideal place for walking, sipping and supping; further south, Burgundy in France or Chianti in Tuscany are two more. In autumn the vines hang heavy with grapes and the leaves turn a rich rust colour.

In many regions the villages are also an attractive feature of the landscape, perched on an unlikely hilltop or tumbling down a headland. Massed whitewashed villas by the Mediterranean or sanctuaries in Tibet, golden stone cottages in the English Cotswolds, thatched pole huts in Laos, or clustered mud-brick dwellings in Morocco can be a true highlight of a walk. A path that wanders from village to village is a wonderful combination of small privations and simple indulgences and a chance to soak up local culture.

URBAN WALKING

Naturally, there is much 'culture' to be found in towns and cities. One of the many attractions of walking the pilgrimage route from

Le Puy to Conques in southern France is the number of charming towns along the way, studded with fine examples of Romanesque architecture. I have nothing against walking in city centres—we rarely forgo the chance to explore interesting ones *en route*—but you will find that walking in remote and lightly populated areas does diminish your taste for permanent massed gatherings. Some cities are more walkable than others. Our local one, Sydney, is a huge, sprawling city that can be enjoyed by walking its coastal edge. We recently spent a week walking its shores from north to south and largely skirted suburbia and commerce. Instead, we were rewarded with secluded beaches, wind-sculpted rock platforms, views of plunging cliffs, plus interesting architecture and iconic structures such as the spinnaker Opera House and coat-hanger Harbour Bridge.

A few tips when walking in a city centre:

- Wear your boots: paved streets are hard on the feet and cobble-stones doubly so.
- Dump your full pack at a hotel or rail station and carry only a day-pack.
- Get hold of a city map and plot out a rough route before starting off; you don't have to stick to it slavishly.
- Consider the underlying topography: for example, a city normally grows up by a river that you can use for orientation.
- Climb bell-towers or high monuments to get the lie of the land.
- As well as visiting the popular sites, explore any lanes or alleys that look interesting.

- When you're weary (and you will be sooner than usual), seek out a park or botanic garden for some green peace.

Your specific interests might be the basis for choosing a place to walk or for determining your route within a region. We once met an amateur bell-ringer walking between villages with historic church bells that he wished to sound. John became particularly excited when he found a *souterrain* marked on a Scottish map and made it the destination for a lengthy walk. It turns out that a souterrain is not an ancient throne of ancestral souters but an underground passage, or in this case, an overgrown jumble of rocks in the middle of a field. Still, the walk was entirely pleasant.

We also take the opportunity to walk through cemeteries and visit tombs along the way; how a culture deals with death is always interesting. The ancient Lycians lodged their dead in elaborate miniature houses—complete with pitched roofs, lintels and tiny doors—carved into rockfaces along the Mediterranean coast of Turkey. Walkers in Tibet, on the other hand, may witness a 'sky burial' in which the dead are returned to the natural world, courtesy of birds of prey. Whatever the manner of disposal, such sites are a poignant reminder to us to make the very most of the day's walk!

Some people are beguiled by cultures that are exotic, some enjoy a walk back into history, and others walk in search of places where nature is less heavily marked. Now, the only question is where, precisely . . .

5. Where in the world?

......

With irritating frequency, when someone hears that I'm a keen long-distance walker, I'm asked if I've 'done the pilgrimage walk'. They are inevitably referring to the route that many pilgrims traditionally took from Saint-Jean-Pied-de-Port in France, over the Pyrenees, through several cities, to Santiago de Compostela on the north-west coast of Spain to venerate the purported relics of St James. While this path has a fascinating history and some scenic sections, *it is not the only long walk*. Nor is it the only pilgrimage walk. It was known in Spain as 'the French path' because it was the route most French pilgrims took. The Portuguese arrived from quite a different direction and the English simply caught a boat to La Coroña and strolled the short distance from there. Most of the English didn't bother, though; they had their own sites to visit, such as the tomb of Thomas à

Becket at Canterbury. The non-Christian world certainly wasn't interested, being otherwise concerned with a *hajj* to Mecca or with seeking *moksha* at Hindu sites.

Without detracting from the Camino de Santiago, there's no good reason why walkers—whether of a religious bent or not—should follow the herd (and there are thousands each summer) and choose this particular walk over other, more scenic and less populated routes. Long-distance paths for walkers, with or without a spiritual angle, have been established all over the world and you can choose from a wide range of lengths, terrains and cultural experiences. I suspect if people knew what else is on offer, there would be fewer tormented souls plodding through stifling heat across the wheat-covered plains of northern Spain.

How do you find out about all those other classic walks? As a starting point, peruse some of the inspirational books of 'great treks' on the large-format shelf at your library. They seldom provide sufficient details to actually undertake the journey, but they give a wonderful insight into many and varied footpaths dotted around the globe. That said, our first book on walking— boldly titled *Classic Walks in Western Europe*—was an attempt to cover both bases with numerous photographs as well as detailed walk notes. Whether or not it fulfilled our ambitious aim, we had a great deal of fun researching it.

Several websites provide a summary of worldwide walking opportunities: have a wander through the American one known as GORP (Great Outdoor Recreation Pages) or others listed at the back of this book. Most countries with national parks have a government website providing information and useful links.

While you're on the internet, browse through websites of the many companies that organise walks. Even if you have no intention of walking with a group of strangers, their programs will point you to beautiful spots that have a network of walking paths; it's a fair bet that if several walk-providers go to the same place then that place is worth going to. Similarly, mapping organisations will have paper or online catalogues that include large-scale maps of areas of particular natural value for recreational use. We have a wonderful map produced by IGN showing all the GRs (*grandes randonnées* or long-distance paths) of France which shows, at a glance, the regions where many paths converge.

Many would-be walkers will be lured by the exotic. If you have a passion for all things Spanish—cuisine, music, siestas—then you'll be looking for a trek in Spain, if only to walk off all that *tapas*. Some will wish to sample cultures that are even more foreign to them. Such countries may or may not have an infrastructure for walkers: this depends on factors such as population density, whether the nation is sufficiently wealthy to have a culture of walking for leisure, or whether it has sufficient attractions to create a trekking industry. As a general rule, the less developed the country, the more help you will gain from a walking-tour operator who can deal with local languages, transport arrangements, permits, porters and supplies. Lonely Planet publishes books specifically on walking in countries where the pastime is practicable and popular. Among the more general travel guides, Rough Guides are the most inclined to include ideas for walkers.

The world is waking up to the attractions of walking, whether as participants or as hosts. Many tourists see only the most polished facet of a culture and their only contact with locals is with hotel staff and ticket sellers. Travellers on foot are more exposed to the rhythm of daily life in smaller communities and have a better chance of striking up a conversation, albeit limited: many of our longer encounters have been with people working in the fields or herding livestock. Shopkeepers in quiet villages are often up for a chat as well. Watching a game of pétanque or of cards in the village square is a good way to become involved in a quiet way and you might even be invited to join in. Where the culture is very different from your own, a local guide can explain aspects of local life and act as an interpreter with villagers along the way.

Over time, people who live on the most frequently trodden routes will become less curious about outsiders, which is a good reason to make your own journey and not follow everyone else across the north of Spain. Just make sure you also avoid any unpleasant domestic turmoil and skirt the border regions between warring nations. A country, of course, is an artificial concept, and one of the great delights of a long walk is the chance to cross borders, or to stand astride one, well away from officialdom. Assuming you do have all the necessary paperwork, here, in a couple of thousand words, is a whirlwind tour of the wayfarer's world.

WESTERN EUROPE

Despite its increasing economic unity, this part of the world is crammed with diverse cultures and its settlements are thoughtfully spaced a day's walk apart, spanning landscapes that range from the intricately cultivated to the breathtakingly wild. Ancient footpaths that once served traders and herders are now tended, charted and waymarked for the pleasure of walkers. If, like me, you prefer a degree of comfort at night and want to walk independently, this is an obvious destination.

Britain is rich in varied landscapes, from the wild north-west of Scotland to the well-tended south of England, and planning a walk is ridiculously easy for the English speaker (although some of the dialects can be thrillingly incomprehensible). Tempting though it might be, you should resist the urge to plan a walking excursion solely on the basis of quaint place names. Britain does offer a wealth of landmarks that are beguiling to both the eye and ear—Dungeon Ghyll, Strumble Head, Nibley Knoll, to say nothing of delightfully unpronounceable Welsh and Gaelic names—but there are places that do not live up to their names and you do not want to waste shoe leather to discover this. Take advantage of the numerous official long-distance paths (or LDPs) that will lead you through quaintly named localities in the Lake District, Cotswolds, Yorkshire Dales, Scottish Highlands, Welsh Brecon Beacons and along the south-west coast. In Britain, walking is not so much a pastime as a natural religion. Plus there are pubs serving real ale to make the wayfaring even more pleasurable.

Ireland has a rich Celtic heritage and lush green landscapes thanks to plentiful rain, with many walking paths for exploring its low mountains, such as the Wicklows, and its rugged western coastline on the Dingle Peninsula or the Ring of Kerry. Of Europe's other islands, Iceland is perhaps the most wild, offering a limited number of paths through geologically vibrant landscapes.

Be prepared to carry extra gear and to ford icy streams, but in summer you'll have plenty of daylight in which to do it. Walkers on Corsica, Sardinia or Crete will enjoy a decidedly warmer climate and discover a rural life that is more challenging than elsewhere in Europe. Corsica's well-maintained paths will lead you from sparkling seas to mountainous ridgelines in a matter of days.

France has a vast network of paths, including the aforementioned *grandes randonnées*, concentrated in the rolling hills of the Massif Central where the major rivers spring, and in the south-east where the Alps rise, or south-west by the Pyrenees. The Pyrenees can be traversed from coast to coast on the GR10, while the French Alps can be negotiated via the ultra-long GR5 or its several branch paths. Away from the mountains, walkers in France can fuel up on fine food and wine and walk through a landscape rich in history, art and architecture, whether chateau-hopping along the Loire or tracking the turbulent Cathar heresy in the south-west. John and I have written a really useful and well-illustrated guide called *Walking France*.

Italy's official long-distance paths are mostly in the north among the Alps and the remarkable Dolomites, but further south the options for walking from village to village offer an irresistible combination of culture and setting. Apart from having only modest-sized mountains, Umbria has it all: charming vineyards and olive groves, Roman temples, teetering hill towns and numerous Renaissance frescoes. The whole countryside is littered with signs of ancient and medieval civilisation and the generous Italians are delighted to share it all with you. It even has stunning coastal walking near Amalfi and along Liguria's now-renowned Cinque Terre. Oh, there's a very helpful book called *Walking Italy*, and here ends the shameless self-promotion.

There are more good spirits (including port and sherry) further west. Portugal's vine-terraced Douro Valley is a popular destination for walkers, as is its Peneda-Gerês national park. Spain has the overwalked Camino plus more exciting walking in its mountain ranges, including the Pyrenees, the limestone Picos de Europa and the Sierra Nevada near Grenada, where Moorish influences are evident in the whitewashed villages. In the south, be prepared for a land of contrasts where arid hillsides are contoured to reveal lush groves of almonds and fruit trees.

Switzerland is, as Ernest Hemingway described it, 'a small, steep country, much more up and down than sideways' and offers a lifetime of exquisite alpine walking along well-maintained paths; indeed, walking is *the* reason for visiting Switzerland. Austria is like Switzerland with shorter mountains, but with better beer and a richer musical heritage: the lake district near Salzburg is particularly fine. Germans are prodigious hikers and so obsessively marked paths are found anywhere there are hills, particularly in the *Schwarzwald* (Black Forest) and Bavarian Alps.

The Scandinavian countries are replete with lakes, mountains and fjords but with an unfortunately short walking season. In northern Finland you can follow the famous Karhunkierros, a path that circles past cliffs and gorges of Oulanka National Park, with huts along the way. For more extended walking, you might consider the long-distance Susitaival or Karhunpolku, which translate somewhat ominously as the Wolf's Trail and the Bear's

Path. There are numerous long paths in Sweden, the most popular being the Kungsleden or King's Way up in the north. Norway boasts even greater variety, with particularly spectacular walks among the jagged spires of the Jotunheim range, the Home of the Giants. Scenery and history combine in the pilgrimage route of St Olav's Way, from Oslo to Trondheim.

For the ultra-keen, eleven long-distance routes (E-paths) currently crisscross continental Europe, from Estonia to Portugal, and Sweden to Greece, giving ample border-hopping opportunities. On the more manageable Tour of Mont Blanc, walkers can sample three countries in a matter of days.

EASTERN EUROPE AND CENTRAL ASIA

Eastern Europe also has a historic network of paths, and as countries become more urbanised there's an increasing interest in walking for leisure. The Alps extend into Slovenia, which has excellent hut-to-hut walking and guides published in English. The Czech Republic has a well-maintained network of paths for exploring the meadows and fairytale castles of Moravia and Bohemia. For those who hungered to walk in Transylvania after seeing either Werner Herzog's or F.W. Murnau's version of *Nosferatu the Vampyre*, those mountain scenes were more likely shot in the High Tatras in the Slovakian part of the Carpathians. In the foothills of the Romanian Carpathians, however, you can walk from little-changed village to village on foot. Further south in Bulgaria, you can walk hut to hut in the glacially carved Pirin Mountains, visiting remote monasteries along the way. Turkey now has two official long-distance walks that pass by the remains of ancient settlements and present-day hamlets. The Kaçkar range in north-east Turkey is home to a mix of ethnic groups and to some serious mountain passes between villages.

Central Asia generally resists the attention of independent walkers, although commercial operators are venturing into Kyrgyzstan, Mongolia and other remote destinations. The Altai Mountains in western Mongolia can be explored with assistance from camels and a trekking company. The mecca for walking, however, is undoubtedly the Himalaya—the youngest and highest of the world's mountains, which have long been the destination of various pilgrimages. Organised trekking, which began in Nepal, is now also well established in India, Bhutan, Pakistan, Tibet and Sikkim. In Nepal it's possible to trek staying at lodges or tea-houses; in most other regions, you'll need to camp, whether independently or as a group. Many countries require trekkers to have permits and control their numbers with high fees; in Bhutan, only treks organised by registered companies are permitted. In addition to the awe-inspiring scenery, trekkers in the Himalaya encounter cultures a world away from their own—the landscape is dotted with small settlements making use of every flat space and some not-so-flat bits. The people are extremely friendly and the chance to visit a Buddhist *gompa* or to drink *rakshi* with the locals only adds to the experience.

AUSTRALASIA AND THE OTHER BITS OF ASIA

Australia, the oldest continent, is sparsely populated, adding a degree of difficulty to bushwalking over long distances. Self-sufficient hikers can traverse dramatic landscapes on the Larapinta Trail or walk through magnificent forest on the longer Bibbulmun Track. Carnarvon Gorge features ancient Aboriginal rock art and there is more stunning gorge walking in the Kimberley. There are a number of trails across low mountains such as the Flinders and MacDonnell Ranges and in the highest range—the Australian Alps—old drovers' huts serve as basic shelters. You can enjoy long coastal walks in most of the states and on Hinchinbrook Island off northern Queensland. There's plenty of good centre-based walking in the Blue Mountains near Sydney or at the Warrumbungles further north-west. Tasmania has some walkers' huts along with lots of stunning terrain: mountainous, forest and coastal. The well-maintained Overland Track is especially rewarding.

New Zealand, a compact patchwork of landscapes, is even better organised for tramping, with hundreds of huts and many official 'Great Walks' such as the Routeburn, the Milford, and the Abel Tasman Coast Track. My favourite walk there so far (though not rated as a 'Great Walk' because the hut facilities are simpler) is the route up the Rees River and down the Dart River.

Closer to the equator, in Papua New Guinea, the historic Kokoda Trail is a strenuous (and often muddy) trek that can be walked independently or with assistance.

Further east, Borneo offers walking in equatorial rainforest (watch out for leeches) and the chance to stay in traditional longhouses or to trek up South-East Asia's highest peak, Mount Kinabalu. In Thailand, Vietnam and Laos it's possible to walk in rainforest and over low mountains, staying in the villages of local hill tribes and mingling with vibrantly costumed people on market days. A more arduous trek takes you to the summit of Fansipan in northern Vietnam, the highest peak on the Indochina peninsula. Further north, Yunnan province in China has spectacular scenery amid the Meili Snow Mountains. More of this vast and diverse country will no doubt be opened up to walkers over time.

Away from the cities, mountainous Japan has many well-maintained trails in its various national parks, most notably in the Hida Range in central Honshu. On isolated Hokkaido, there is wild volcanic walking on the peninsula of Shiretoko, which translates as End of the Earth. Nearer to civilisation, around Kyoto, walkers can follow paths built during the feudal period and stop at old post-road stations where traditional Japanese hospitality is still shown.

NORTH AMERICA

North Americans have a strange relationship with the outdoors. Vast tracts of wild landscapes are protected in national parks, created when the real frontier was slipping away, but they are difficult to access. Dozens of trails traverse the continent but to hike long sections you must play the role of the rugged pioneer, carrying all gear and camping out with night-prowling bears. Accommodation is limited to the occasional isolated lodge catering to hunters, anglers and would-be cowboys, rather than walkers. There are exceptions—the Appalachian Mountain Club has a system of staffed refuges, and the Alpine Club of Canada operates huts in the national parks of Alberta and British Columbia—but they are few and literally far between. Elsewhere you'll need to be self-sufficient or walk with a guided group; organised adventures often make use of vehicle support to link up a series of day-walks.

As a consolation, independent walkers will discover plenty of centre-based walking, particularly in the west, which has an unfair share of natural wonders. Yosemite Valley, in the Sierra Nevada, was much loved by early environmentalist John Muir. I have amazing memories of day-walks there, as well as in nearby Zion and Bryce Canyon National Parks, with my family when I was young. The Grand Canyon is another natural wonder and can be admired from the level Rim Trail or explored via various paths that drop to the canyon floor. Wyoming's Grand Tetons offer walkers a taste of the southern Rockies and is less crowded than Yellowstone National Park. Even less crowded are the trails in Alaska, with rewarding walking near Anchorage or Juneau.

In the USA's east, there are good footpaths in the Adirondacks and the White Mountains (the latter with huts). The North Country Trail, currently being developed, links scenic areas of great diversity.

Canada has a trio of proximate national parks in Jasper, Banff and Yoho, all with excellent paths for day-walks. It also has some fine coastal walking, including the West Coast Trail on Vancouver Island and a wealth of routes on Nova Scotia, where a heritage of Scottish, French and Irish migrants is combined with that of the Micmac Indians.

SOUTH AMERICA

Every climatic zone is on offer in South America, from tropical jungle to soaring mountains, plus a great diversity of cultures ranging from the very European Argentina to the indigenous cultures of Peru and Bolivia. Assisted walking is available in many regions, relying often on pack animals and their handlers. Glacier-cloaked Patagonia in the far south has a brief walking season and a few refuges along paths below the dramatic Torres del Paine and Fitz Roy granite peaks (both are on my list for hiking in the near future). There are trails through spectacular Andean scenery further north, in Bolivia, Peru and Ecuador. The most famous of these is the Inca Trail, which ascends through jungle and cloud forest to the ancient ruins of Machu Picchu. Numbers on the Inca Trail are now limited and the path is closed for part of the year, but you can follow other walking paths to arrive at the same destination. For the hardy, routes through the Cordillera Blanca and the Cordillera Huayhuash cross numerous high passes in the Peruvian Andes. Trekking companies also offer jungle walking in the Table Mountains of Venezuela. On a jungle trek into Brazil's Xixua-Xiparin reserve you may encounter giant otters, howler monkeys and anacondas.

AFRICA AND THE MIDDLE EAST

Southern Africa has a tradition of 'trailing', but permits are required for many routes as they often cross private land. South Africa boasts numerous wonderful hiking trails with the added attraction of huts along the way (a 1980 guidebook lists which ones are to be used by 'Whites' and which ones by 'Coloureds and Asians'). Among the choices are challenging mountain walks in the Drakensberg, a hike through Namibia's spectacular Fish River Canyon, or a gentle stroll through the vineyards of the

South African Cape. My youngest nephew Al has just returned from a guided hike on the large island of Madagascar, filled with tales of camping in schoolyards (complete with playful schoolkids) and sightings of chameleons and lemurs. Back on the mainland, hiking in central Africa is focused on Kilimanjaro—the world's highest freestanding mountain, which can be trekked up by the fit. Or you might prefer a mid-level trek to encircle Mount Kenya or a strenuous trek into Uganda's high Rwenzori range. Across the continent, there is breathtaking walking between the escarpment-perched villages of the Dogon people in Mali. In the far north, it's possible to walk between Berber villages nestled among the High Atlas mountains of Morocco. The rock-hewn countrysides of Jordan and Iran all have rich landscapes that can be explored on foot, made more accessible with the help of trekking companies.

If you are bewildered by choice it is worth remembering several points. Firstly, this will probably not be your only big walk. Secondly, your own tastes and frame of mind can greatly affect the charm of any place. Finally, recall the adage of Paddy Pallin, a pioneer of Australian bushwalking: 'The only trips I regret are the ones I did not do.'

6. Planning an itinerary

......

The much-travelled writer Robert Dessaix has suggested, somewhat archly, that

> we tend to concentrate less on being where we go than on planning for it, photographing it and then endlessly recounting it to people who basically don't want to know about it, except as an element in their own plans for planning and photographing and recounting.

I'm not disputing the truth of this, but does it matter terribly? As long as we don't misuse the time spent being where we go, is there any harm in drawing the greatest possible enjoyment from a journey, both before and after? I'll touch on the acts of photographing and recounting towards the end of this book, but I'm happy to admit here and now that I take great pleasure in the planning of a walking trip. The joys are manifold: there's the task of narrowing down a whole world of possibilities, the hunt for maps and guides, the study of these mysterious documents to assess what's feasible, the search for obscure modes of transport, the collation of map segments and track notes and, finally, the packing—which is so much fun that I've left it for a later chapter. All this anticipation and preparation is part and parcel of a journey by foot.

Some people will consider my level of planning too regimented and restrictive, leaving little room for spontaneity and chaotic adventure. Too much spontaneity, however, and those critics may find themselves benighted on the side of a mountain. If you have three months set aside for wandering, detailed planning isn't such an issue. I personally don't have enough time left in life to spend it waiting for a bus that comes along every third day. (This did happen to us once. I misread a French train timetable and we stood waiting on a platform while, unseen, our rail-bus pulled away from the station. It was probably the only occasion holidaymakers have passed any time in St Auban, a drab mining town in the French Alpilles.) By all means, build time into an itinerary that allows for rest or to soak up atmosphere, but know ahead what places are most likely to merit investigation and how they can be reached.

You've already given thought to the style of walking you prefer. If you've opted for a trek with a commercial outfit, you are largely relieved of the joys and burden of planning. You might have to organise travel to and fro, but the details of where you overnight, how you follow the route and where you acquire food will be taken care of. This doesn't mean you should be oblivious to such details; make enquiries if these aren't forthcoming. Now you can skip the rest of this chapter.

If you're not trekking with a commercial operator you will need to decide what sort of route you will take and at what time of year. You'll also want to gather material that will make the experience more interesting and enjoyable. Having ascertained where accommodation is available, you can then rough out a day-by-day itinerary. For one recent trip with friends, we went into greater detail, noting proposed walking times and height gains for each day, along with alternative local transport in case someone opted not to walk that day. Karen, who developed an inexplicable antipathy towards blizzards, made good use of the information.

Near the chapter's end, I'll give an example of another of our itineraries and show how a well-laid plan failed, happily, to correspond with eventuality.

TYPE OF ROUTE

From the earliest days of the first mountaineering club, the Alpine Club, there emerged two types of climbers. There were those who stayed in one village, venturing out to ascend various peaks and returning each evening to the same hotel; they referred to themselves as 'centrists'. The 'ex-centrists' opted to carry more gear—those nineteenth-century ropes were heavy!—and walk long routes over passes, climbing side peaks along the way. These two approaches also apply to walking excursions today.

Day-walks from a base
If you adopt the centrist philosophy and choose one base from which to make day-walks, there are several advantages. The most obvious one is that you can head off each day with a smaller and lighter pack. Your base can be a village, a farm, a hut or a campsite, but it should be located so you can walk a loop in different directions each day, as if drawing the petals of a flower. If you can catch some form of public transport and then walk an interesting route back to your base, you'll see even more. Centrism is a good choice if you're new to this walking business and not entirely sure how much distance you want to cover, or whether you'll enjoy walking every day.

Centre-based stays are also a good idea in mountain areas where the weather is very changeable; if the forecast doesn't look good, you can stay snug with a good book. (Sir Leslie Stephen's account of climbing the Rothhorn in the Swiss Alps included a lengthy description of the inn from which they mounted their expedition, including details of the sofa: 'The minute criticism of M. Epinay's establishment is due to the fact that we spent there three days of enforced idleness.') The best town or village bases for mountain walking have an excellent infrastructure of transport—shuttles, funicular railways, chairlifts, and so on—or are at the confluence of two or more valleys, opening up walks in several directions. The choice of high-level walks versus valley walking can be guided by the day's weather forecast. Hard walks can be interspersed with easy alternatives.

We've enjoyed extended stays in such mountain towns as Cauterets in the Pyrenees, Cortina d'Ampezzo in the Dolomites,

Cogne in Italy's Gran Paradiso, and Lauterbrunnen in the Bernese Alps of Switzerland. High villages with a great deal of character have served us well: Hallstatt in Austria's Salzkammergut and Bonneval-sur-Arc in the French Vanoise. In North America, a lodge in Glacier or Yellowstone National Park would make a fine base.

Away from the mountains, centre-based walking is also possible in compact areas that are rich in interest: Italy's Cinque Terre could easily be explored this way by staying in Monterosso. In Australia, you might station yourself at Katoomba in the Blue Mountains, but the ideal Australian base will often be a campsite in a national park.

The long-distance path

The alternative—walking from A to B—is known to Americans as a 'through hike'. It requires a heavier pack but it does give you a greater sense of purpose, of going somewhere. It is also a great deal easier to boast about later, when you're recounting your tales to Robert Dessaix and friends. 'We walked from Chamonix to Zermatt' sounds much more impressive than 'we pottered around in the Swiss Alps'.

Of course, there's not much point walking from A to B (or even A and back to A in a circuit or tour) if the bit in between lacks charm. To be fully assured of a sustained scenic walk, stick to the established 'long-distance paths' that have a name: the Cotswold Way in England, the Milford Track in New Zealand or the Otter Trail in South Africa. If you're prepared to do extra planning, however, you can make up your own long-distance path by studying detailed maps and linking up existing paths. If it proves a success, you can always give it a suitably grand title: the Tour de Provence or the Western Fjords Trail.

The term 'long-distance path' is applied to anything that can't be walked in a single day, but can also denote something much, much longer. North America is full of trails that extend to thousands of kilometres, such as the Appalachian Trail (3460 km) or the Pacific Crest Trail (4260 km). In Europe, you can walk from the North Sea to the Mediterranean, the Baltic to the Adriatic, or follow other E-paths from country to country. Presumably such epic routes will have their high points and quite a few low points, and those who undertake such a walk in its entirety are either tenacious or obsessive in the extreme. There is something of the 'completist' in all of us, though, and length is relative. My 80-year-old father, walking for a week with me in England, refused point-blank to catch a local bus when he was clearly weary; he had come to walk the Ridgeway and that's what he was going to do.

Some walkers choose to hike the full length of a long-distance path, but in sections, completing a stage each summer holiday. This is feasible if the path is not too far from home, but if it's on the other side of the world, you're better off selecting the most interesting section. We've particularly enjoyed the second half of the Scottish West Highland Way and, on another trip, the first ten days—from Le Puy to Conques—on the French route to Compostela. A guidebook for a long-distance path will usually alert you to the best stretches. (On a related subject, remember that following a historic route slavishly can lead you across golf courses and through newly sprung suburbia, so use your discretion and adjust your route for modernity.)

Walking a circuit or tour gives you the option of returning to a car or of leaving excess luggage at your starting/finishing point. Rail or bus stations used to be the place to do this; now, with tighter security measures, a hotel is a more likely storage location. If you do leave luggage somewhere, label the outside with your name and date of return, otherwise someone might feel the need to detonate it.

HOW FAR AND HOW LONG?

The Victorians, as mentioned earlier, were prodigious walkers. G.M. Trevelyan claimed that the life-enhancing moments that a walker seeks 'come to me only after five-and-twenty miles'. Most people would find that distance too vivifying by half, but this raises the issues of pace and pattern: do you wish to amble or to lope? To walk long days or short ones? You might want to dawdle along the way, taking time to concentrate on 'being where you are', or you might prefer a brisk tempo. You might, quite sensibly, prefer to walk only for half-days, so as to enjoy the ambience of a village or the drama of a mountain setting, or to read and relax in the afternoon. That's not for everyone: when, on rare occasions, we arrive at our destination early, we inevitably go for another long stroll, liberated of packs.

The other matter to be settled is how many days of walking you will enjoy. Early on in your walking career (and it will probably become a career!) you may think anything more than a week sounds an exceedingly long time to spend on foot, but this concern will shortly evaporate. The daily pattern of walking soon becomes self-perpetuating, like a percussive beat. If you're tackling a long-distance path, consider how the route can be broken down (referring to estimated walking times rather than distances) to suit your ideal distance per day, and then your ideal number of days so as to reach civilisation once more.

Allow time to ease into a walk: the first couple of days are often the hardest and it would be terrible to abandon the whole endeavour simply because your muscles haven't read the itinerary. Allow the occasional uncommitted day in scenic spots for either rest, harsh weather or, if all goes well, side walks. In practice you'll find that rest days are actually more hectic than those spent walking. There are clothes to launder, yourself to wash more thoroughly, provisions to be purchased, family to be contacted, possible accommodation to be reserved and, in general, a lot more decisions to be made. It's always a slight relief to be back on the path.

We've found that our ideal duration for a walking 'research trip' is six weeks; after that, I become aware of myriad tiny bones in my feet and my shorts start walking of their own accord. For those with duties and responsibilities, a fortnight or four weeks is more likely the limit of a holiday and you might only wish to walk for part of that time. If time does allow a series of walks, mix up the terrain—perhaps a coastal route followed by a tour through vineyards in Europe, or jungle then mountains in Peru—but avoid having to travel huge distances between adventures. Stopovers with friends or relatives can be both restorative and productive, particularly if they own a washing machine.

WHEN TO GO?

Walkers have a smaller window of opportunity than other travellers. We have to juggle several factors: favourable weather conditions, the most picturesque season and the stiffness of the competition. If you can only get away from work at a certain time of the year, choose a destination that is best at that time; if you're more flexible, you're free to choose the destination first.

In most parts of the world, the ideal walking seasons are the local spring and autumn. However, in places where the temperatures can be oppressively hot, winter might be the best time to walk. Many Australians are required to take leave in the height of summer when the only pleasant walking, for much of the country, is on the coast where there's a breeze and the chance to cool off in the ocean. Luckily, it's also a good time to head to New Zealand. Among European mountains, walkers have to navigate between late-lying snow (especially on high passes) and early snowfall; some high-level huts only open from July to mid-September. We walked the Tour of Mont Blanc over the second half of June, often arriving just after a hut had opened for the season and with the luxury of a bunkroom to ourselves. In monsoon-affected Nepal, the trekking season is roughly October to April. In central Africa, the walking is best from December to March or from June to September. Study the programs of trekking companies: either edge of their season for a particular walk should offer a compromise of good weather and a quieter path.

Local school holidays and peak tourist seasons are unlikely to spoil your time on the footpath, but they may make it harder to find a bed. If seeking a degree of solitude, walk mid-week when there will be fewer day-walkers, and try not to be on well-known stretches of path on holiday weekends. If possible, plan to walk when others will be occupied elsewhere—say in front of the television watching the Olympics or some other mass distraction. If undertaking a popular long walk, avoid starting on a Saturday, when other people will have the same idea. Also be aware of religious observations that might interrupt day-to-day business in certain countries. Festivals often draw large numbers of tourists (bad), but obscure local ones can add to the interest of a walk (good). We once caught the Festival of Soup in Florac, France, which was a lot less interesting than the one we stumbled across in Cogne, in the Italian Alps. At the latter, pregnant cows of the district competed in a shoving contest in the *Batailles de Reines*; at the former, we ate soup.

In most countries, the season for wildflowers happily coincides with a good walking temperature. While this makes spring attractive, those walking in temperate climates where deciduous trees put on a colourful display are also in for a treat in autumn. If you plan to walk long days, check how many hours of daylight you'll get in a particular season. Finally, budget-conscious travellers should make a point of knowing when airlines tweak up prices; the edge of shoulder season holds a certain appeal for us.

GATHERING INFORMATION

You've chosen where you want to walk, in what manner and when. You've paid close attention when listening to the tales of returned travellers, à la Dessaix, and quizzed friends who've walked the path or region that interests you. The guidebooks that helped you select a destination included sections on local culture, history and natural features such as flora and fauna. You may even have unearthed insightful literary works that you have every intention of reading before you go but probably won't until you return. Now you need to collect nuggets of practical information regarding networks of walking paths, the availability of food, water and shelter, and details of transport to and fro. You'll also want a map and an indication of how much navigating will be needed.

The naive traveller would assume that a tourist office would prove helpful at this point. Sadly, few tourist offices at national or regional level have provided us with useful path information apart from accommodation listings. At the local level it is pot luck. Some of the least helpful people I have ever encountered have been in the employ of tourist offices: they spot a blob of mud on your boots or catch a glint off your water flask and treat your enquiries with all the disdain they can muster. Presumably it's the realisation that you're unlikely to lavish money on nearby multi-star hotels or indulge in expensive spa treatments that creates this animosity. There are exceptions, thank goodness, and you might be blessed with a tourist officer who actually enjoys a walk and is pleased to dig out that rare leaflet on local footpaths. If so, give that person a kiss on behalf of all the walking fraternity.

Track notes

If you're heading to an area preserved as a national park or reserve, search on the internet for an official website. These often include details of short walks that can be adapted and reinterpreted for more ambitious purposes. If you're requesting information, explain that you are happy to walk for a full day and can navigate. (If you can't navigate, read Chapter 11 in this book first.) New Zealand's Department of Conservation, which manages walking trails, has a wonderful website for walkers, providing sketch maps, walking times and online booking for huts. In some countries you may have to arrange a permit to walk in certain parks.

The internet is a boon for planning long walks. Numerous sites act as directories for hikers, with links to more specific sites across the world. Some long-distance paths even have their own dedicated website, promoting facilities along the trail and suggesting ways to break the route into stages. There are, for example, websites for the Coast-to-Coast and West Highland Way in Britain, the Tour of Mont Blanc in Europe and the Inca Trail in Peru. When searching a walk by name, you'll discover that there are also plenty of descriptions posted by individual enthusiasts. These range from the didactic to the inane. Countries with a culture of walking generally have a national hiking organisation, such as The Ramblers in Britain. These groups, as well as clubs for mountaineers, have websites that have useful path information or offer links to further websites that do; see the back of this book for addresses that include English translations. The site of the French walking body, the FFRP, remains cruelly untranslated.

I still like referring to books, as a lot of effort will have gone into their content. There are quite a few English-language publishers producing hiking guides: Cicerone Press publishes guides to specific regions and is particularly strong on Europe; Lonely Planet has a range of titles on walking in different countries;

Trailblazer guides cover the classic walking regions and routes and include excellent sketch maps. The FFRP in France has a huge range of detailed guides to routes in France, but very few have been translated. Such guidebooks suggest route stages, estimate walking times, summarise accommodation options, and provide detailed track notes. They are surprisingly reliable, but you should note the date of publication as things change over time.

Locating maps

While large-scale maps are useful for getting an overview of a country or region, you will need detailed maps for walking. Even if you're on an official waymarked route, a map is invaluable for knowing what's to come and for interpreting what you're seeing. If you're exploring an area on day-walks from a centre, a scale of 1:25,000 is ideal. If you're walking through on a long-distance trail, a scale of 1:50,000 is more sensible (or else you'll need too many maps), as long as the path is waymarked and navigation won't be a constant concern.

The sooner you can lay your hands on such maps, the better. Don't assume one will be available where the trail starts. Friends once spent a full day in Buenos Aires trying to track down detailed Patagonian maps and eventually located them at a military office. Most cities have a map shop that can order particular maps for you. Alternatively, several online map-sellers are listed at the back of this book and you can use their websites (or go direct to a country's mapping authority) to peruse which maps you will need. Better still if you can borrow them from a friend! Some guidebooks contain detailed topographical maps that render a separate map unnecessary; these are particularly useful for a long linear walk where you'd otherwise have to buy numerous expensive maps. For a few popular routes you can buy a strip map that achieves the same thing.

Having obtained the relevant map, you can use it to plan stages and find shelter along the way. If your only experience to date is with street directories, you will come across a few map-reading tips in Chapter 11, 'Finding the way'.

Accommodation

If you're not taking a tent and will be relying on local hospitality, you need to know in advance where it will be offered. The only time our planning failed severely was on the Vercors Plateau in France, for which we had difficulty sourcing information. What snippets we did get proved out of date and we had to change our route as we went, as John refused to sleep in a burnt-out hut. Happily that has improved: friends recently brought back a wonderful Vercors walking map issued freely—oh wonders!—by the regional tourist office.

Once we have plotted a route, I note down settlements of any size and any remote hostels or huts as marked on the map. Next I create a grid with columns for location, establishment, sleeping options (dorm or own room), tariffs, meals served, telephone and email. Then, I rummage through books and search on the internet, combining each place name with hut/gîte/albergo/refuge as appropriate, hunting for details of each accommodation provider and filling in the grid. It's painstaking work and that's why John lets me do it.

I avoid websites for booking hotels as these generally list only more expensive hotels in towns, and rarely smaller inns in the countryside. It's amazing what you can find, though. When planning for the Swiss Walkers' Haute Route I found that refuges along one section would not yet be open for the season—so I trawled the internet and discovered, just a short detour off the path, a hotel with a dormitory. We four were the only guests in an isolated, six-storey concrete tower that once housed workers building the Lac des Dix dam; Le Ritz (truly) was a little surreal, but much appreciated. Even if you have a guidebook listing accommodation along a route, some places will have closed, new ones opened, and others still may have opening dates that vary from year to year. Hut guardians can have the discretion to close early for the season if patronage is thin. If you've found an email address but little else, you can quickly send a request for more information. If all you have is a phone number, note down a few relevant words, telephone at an appropriate hour and you'll probably find sufficient common language to cover the essentials.

You can also make a reservation if you think this is necessary. I only reserve well ahead on the most popular routes. John thought it a sad sign of ageing and increasing risk aversion when I booked along the Coast-to-Coast in England—until we met people who were making elaborate detours off the path to find a bed each night. On less well-known paths or routes of our own devising, we carry with us my grid of accommodation options and either make a phone call each morning or simply arrive on a doorstep. We get a few raised eyebrows but have never yet had to bivouac unexpectedly. If you're in an area that draws many holidaymakers, it's wise to reserve during the summer vacation. Along some routes—the 'Great Walks' in New Zealand for example—it's compulsory to reserve a bed or campsite in the high season. Australia's Overland Track and Great Ocean Walk have similar conditions for camping sites, so as to control the numbers of walkers passing through and prevent overcrowding.

Transport between walks

We never use a car for getting to and fro a long walk when abroad. It's not that we're eco-warriors, it's just that we argue too much over directions (also an issue on the path but less dangerous at walking pace). Moreover, a rental car would sit idle for all the time we're on foot. Most walks can be accessed by a combination of rail and local bus. We make use of post buses (once by crouching in a panel van with the sacks of mail), school buses (often smoky), funiculars and tub-sized ferries. Rail routes and timetables are easy to research on the internet; most countries have a national website. The rest will require a bit more searching. Download and print all relevant timetables, along with the key to symbols. If you will be using public transport to return to a starting point, plan to begin with the transport option and then walk back, rather than the other way around. This reduces the impact of misreading a timetable and avoids having to rush a walk so as to catch the last bus for the day. If you can find no public transport to the trail head at the end of a road, note down the telephone number for any taxi service in the nearest town.

A LOOSE ITINERARY

The culmination of all this computer gazing, page flipping and note scribbling should be a rough daily schedule of your walking excursion, from departing home to—all things going well—your return. It might include travel details, overnight stops and possible accommodation, estimates of walking times and distances.

What follows is an annotated example from our early days as guide-writers. To give a little background information, some years previously we had made a brief visit to the Verdon Gorge in Provence, said to be Europe's deepest gorge. With little time and no preparation, we reached the rim of the gorge . . . and had to keep travelling. So this time we were keen to follow a section of the GR4 path that runs through the gorge and to write up a chapter for our first book. We would be reasonably track-fit, following a week's walking over rolling hills in Bavaria and five days of walking the aisles at the Frankfurt Book Fair; as a result we had heavy display folders and vaguely business-like clothes that we didn't want to carry. It was October, a good time to walk in sunny Provence. We had a somewhat dated copy of *Walking the French Gorges* by Alan Castle, and a detailed map on which the GR4 route was marked.

Day 1 *Travel by rail from Germany to Nice. Reserve a hotel for after the walk and leave excess luggage there. Catch the Train des Pignes to Entrevaux*

As we transited through Nice, we found a cheap hotel near the railway station and committed our luggage to the somewhat shifty manager, confident there was nothing among it that anyone else would want. The narrow-gauge train pottered up the dramatic Var valley and deposited us at the lovely town of Entrevaux, with its Napoleonic fortifications.

Day 2 *Walk along GR4 from Entrevaux to Soleilhas; 25.5 km, 9 hours of walking*
A longer day than Alan Castle proposed but the accommodation list from the regional tourist office (this was before the internet was much use) indicated there were no longer any options in the hamlets *en route*. It was a lovely walk over autumnal hills, past shrines and sun-bleached settlements. Tiny Soleilhas was a short detour off the GR4; we hadn't reserved a room and the family who ran the only pension were a little bemused by our twilight arrival.

Day 3 *Walk from Soleilhas through Castellane and on to Point Sublime; 33 km, 9 hours of walking*
We knew that we would write this day up as two days' walk due to the distance and because Castellane is an interesting town. We'd visited it before and hiked the section to Point Sublime so we knew what we were up for. I think we telephoned from Castellane and reserved beds in the lone inn (*auberge*) at Point Sublime, memorable for its setting above the Verdon River and for a flavoursome *daube* of wild boar on the half-board menu.

Day 4 *Walk from Point Sublime through the gorge to La Palud; 20 km, 9 hours*
A singular day of walking; the route through the gorge is amazing. At our lunch spot on the riverbank we first met Paul and Gigi,

with whom we've walked on many occasions since. They told us we should stay with them at the Chalet de la Maline, a refuge perched on the lip of the gorge, which we'd wrongly assumed was only for members of the Club Alpin Français. We were pleased to stop there, rather than road-bash for another two hours to La Palud, as it had been a warm day of solid ascents and descents. A drink on the terrace, watching the evening colours on the gorge walls, was a fine way to end it.

Day 5   *A spare day: possible day-walk on the Sentier de l'Imbut*
We had read that access to the gorge can be closed if hydro water is released upstream. That didn't happen, but we were glad we allowed this spare day.

Day 6   *Walk the GR4 to Moustiers-Sainte-Marie, a village wedged high in a ravine against a backdrop of cliffs*
A long walk will rarely unfold as planned. Staying at La Maline we discovered that the footbridge known as the Passerelle de l'Estellie had been washed away in a spring flood, preventing our proposed day-5 side walk along the other riverbank. That evening, over a convivial dinner, it was arranged by our new friends that we get a lift with Emile, a lone walker who had a car, to the opposite side of the canyon and walk the beautiful Sentier de l'Imbut with him. We had a wonderful day: considering Emile had no English, I realised just how much camaraderie a walk can engender. At the end of the day, Emile gave us a lift on to Moustiers, where we shouted drinks (camaraderie is even thicker over *pastis*) to celebrate a thrilling walk through narrow river canyons. The next day we walked the GR4 back to La Palud

(discovering how difficult it is to write track notes in reverse) and caught a bus on day 7 back to Nice.

COLLATING THE PAPERWORK

Once you've gathered all the relevant information, you may well have reams of paper, an array of maps and a shelf of books. Paper weighs a lot so you'll need to reduce this to something manageable. No publisher will have qualms about you copying pages from books you own, so if you don't want to cut sections from a book, scan them, print double-sided if your printer allows, and trim the pages. As well as track notes and details of accommodation and transport, notes on regional flora and fauna are useful for those countries where local leaflets won't be in English. From a foreign-language phrase book, you might copy pages of words concerned with eating and landscape features, plus some phrases for seeking shelter and directional advice. If you are walking a linear route, you might want to scan and print map sections to create your own strip map; we inherited numerous 1:25,000 maps of England from my eccentric uncle Alf and were able to stitch scanned sections into a highly detailed strip map for the Coast-to-Coast walk. Collate all these pieces of paper so you can access the information easily *en route* and, if necessary, discard it once off the path.

Finally, print an extra copy of your itinerary, including any reserved accommodation, and leave it with someone who'll notice if you fail to return.

7. *Keeping company*

......

It's puzzling that many useful books on the topic of hiking fail to acknowledge the importance of company, other than to make the point that it's safer to have some. Even this statement is arguable: if your company is a thrill-seeking, nimble youth who is addicted to dangerous levels of adrenaline then you're more likely to survive without them.

Your choice of company—assuming you choose any—will have greater repercussions for you when walking than during other forms of travel, for you will keep company more closely and be more reliant on each other. You will depend on them for diversion, for shrewd judgement and, quite possibly, for physical assistance. Heed the advice offered to would-be polar explorers by W.C. Sellar and R.J. Yeatman: 'Choose your companions carefully—you may have to eat them.'

GOING SOLO

In *The Art of Travel* Alain de Botton makes the point that when you travel, you inevitably take yourself along. This, he says, is something we tend to overlook when anticipating a journey; it's only when our usual mental preoccupations and physical limitations prevent us from losing ourselves in our new surroundings that the harsh reality of being permanently attached to a brain and a body sinks in.

I would suggest that on a long walk this phenomenon is intensified: there are bound to be stages—when the scenery shifts slowly or lacks great interest—when you will spend a lot of time with yourself. (For your own sake I hope that you're good company.) However, I suspect that the prolific de Botton hasn't had time to strike out on a really long walk and get into that zone of non-thought. Robert Louis Stevenson certainly did. The Scotsman thought it possible, by getting into a good stride, to leave yourself behind:

> Uneven walking is not so agreeable to the body, and it distracts and irritates the mind. Whereas, when once you have fallen into an equable stride, it requires no conscious thought from you to keep it up, and yet it prevents you from thinking earnestly of anything else.

Like knitting, he said, it puts you in a state of mind where you can enjoy the world 'as in a cheerful dream'.

William Hazlitt had strong opinions on the matter of company: 'One of the pleasantest things in the world is going a journey; but I like to go by myself. I can enjoy society in a room; but out of doors, nature is company enough for me.' He did qualify this by saying that company can be useful if you're going to see something— ruins or what-not—that can be sensibly discussed. And he did believe company to be an absolute necessity when walking in a foreign country, as too much exotica could overwhelm an English psyche unsupported by like-minded fellowship.

Whether abroad or home, for the sake of safety, it is advisable to have walking companions—someone else who can raise the alarm should you fall off a precipice or become trapped between a rock and a hard place and find it necessary to cut off your hand. When camping, having company makes you less vulnerable to the mischief of strangers, and there's an obvious advantage in sharing the load of communal equipment, such as stove and tent.

If you calculate the risks to be low, a solo walk is a secret pleasure; there will be no one with whom to share the experience but, on the upside, you can freely embroider any tales later. Apart from a handful of day-walks, my solo distance walking has been limited to a memorable four days along the Offa's Dyke Path. Offa built his eighth-century defensive dyke along what is now the Welsh border and I followed it, high above the lovely Wye Valley from Chepstow to Hay-on-Wye. So absorbing was the scenery and so engrossing the ruins of Tintern Abbey and the White Castle that I forgot to eat at regular intervals or even, on one day, at all. By the time I got to Hay I was quite peckish and desperate for conversation. Along the way, though, I took new-found pleasure in being able to start, stop and go as I pleased, something Stevenson found irresistible:

A walking tour should be gone upon alone, because freedom is of the essence; because you should be able to stop and go on, and follow this way or that, as the freak takes you; and because you must have your own pace, and neither trot alongside a champion walker, nor mince in time with a girl.

POSSIBLE CANDIDATES

Someone who didn't mind mincing along with a girl was William Wordsworth. According to his biographer Thomas De Quincey, Wordsworth's wife preferred to stay home but his sister Dorothy was 'always ready to walk out', and despite her poor deportment— 'which gave an ungraceful, and even an unsexual character to her appearance when out of doors'—De Quincey grants that she made an admirable walking companion for the poet.

The ideal co-walker is a sympathetic soul—luckily for me, mine happens to be John. The only negative aspect of your life-companion doubling up as your walk-companion is that you have an awful lot of commonality. This means that you can enjoy running jokes (we have jokes that have been distilled over twenty-five years and can now raise a guffaw with a single word), but it also means few fresh opinions crop up unexpectedly. One remedy is to make a point of reading different books.

If they were not soulmates prior to the experience, those who do keep you company on a walk will possibly gain significance in your later life. De Botton suggests that

it's on the basis of shared experiences that intimacy is given an opportunity to grow. Friendships nourished solely by occasional dinners will never have the depth of those forged

on a trek or at university. Two people who are surprised by
a lion in a jungle clearing will, unless one of them is eaten,
be effectively bonded by what they have seen.

Are there lions in jungles? See, I think Alain needs to get out
more.

Conversely, a long walk might dissolve a bond that you
thought cemented. Seemingly harmless habits can become irksome
irritations over time and the constant contact involved in walking
can stretch a friendship a long way. If you're planning a very long
walk, consider asking friends to join you for short sections of it.
Yes, I know I sound like a hard woman, but being pragmatic
will lead to more sustainable friendships. As Mark Twain had
one of his characters say: 'I have found out that there ain't no
surer way to find out whether you like people or hate them than
to travel with them.'

The ties of relatives are stickier: it's in your interest to maintain
good relations, as you're going to bump into them every Christmas.
This is not true of my father, though, who died a few years back.
He was a man who closely guarded his emotions and I'm glad
I had a chance to walk with him in his older age. Not that he
revealed any hidden quarters of his heart; I just felt assured that
I knew him as well as I might. Quite a different phenomenon has
been walking with my nephew Jez. He joined John and me on a
long trip when he was just eighteen and it was a pleasure to watch
him dealing with new experiences while trying to maintain the
insouciance of youth. We all learned new levels of tolerance and
recently he joined us again, this time on a challenging alpine walk.

Happily, he appears to have developed the walking addiction. John will not allow me to invite my brother on long walks as he is inclined to burst into song a little too loudly and a lot too often. He is particularly keen on the Gilbert and Sullivan repertoire.

THE LARGER GROUP

There's an ideal upper limit for numbers in a walking group: it's one where you can get to know each member of the group, not be slowed too much when negotiating obstacles, and each have a voice in decisions. I walk regularly with a local bushwalking club and even on day-walks the group size has a considerable bearing on both practicalities and the general ambience. On overnight hikes, there are added considerations. How much tent space is available, or how many beds are there in the hut? How much impact will we all have on a fragile environment? Worse still, the chance of having a snorer in your midst is greatly increased.

If you're a sociable type, you'll enjoy walking with more than a handful; it allows for a broader range of views and livelier debates on a topic. This is even more likely if you join an organised trek and you're thrown together with strangers from different walks of life. Since you've chosen the same journey, it's likely that your common interests and purpose will be the basis for amiable acquaintance and perhaps even friendship. Good commercial operators limit the size of the group according to the demands and conditions of each route, but fifteen is a common figure. Don't walk with a company that will simply take as many as will fit on a bus. If you can enthuse a group of friends to join you, most companies will provide a walk for a surprisingly small number, perhaps four or six. If you join a group of strangers, make an effort to talk to each individual early on. Not only will this help the group dynamics whereby members look out for each other, but it will help you identify the annoying individual (and there is, inevitably, always one). After that, you can walk quietly on your own without seeming too rude.

MATCH MAKING

Before agreeing to keep someone company on a long walk, you need to ensure that you share similar goals and expectations. You should discuss the general approach you'll take to a walk, whether it will be long and fast, or slow and leisurely. Are you suitably matched for fitness? Nothing could be duller than spending a week sitting and waiting at regular intervals for someone slow . . . and nothing is more soul-destroying than playing tag with people much fitter than you.

In the early stages of a long walk there are bound to be discrepancies, but an underlying chasm between your abilities will remain an issue. In some circumstances, you might be prepared to cope with that gap: walking with my father was a case in point. Charles, for his advanced age, had great stamina, but I empathised with Robert Louis Stevenson, who found it incredibly difficult to match the tedious pace of his recalcitrant donkey Modestine. Interestingly, if I ducked off the track for a quick piss or paused to change a camera lens, my father would apparently tap into a hidden reserve of energy and bolt like lightning down the track so that I was required to trot heavily to catch up, whereupon his pace would decelerate once more.

You're unlikely to find anyone with a pace exactly matching your own—and in truth, it's not necessary. Safety guidelines for walking in a group advise you to keep within eyesight of the person behind and in front, but if the path is well marked I see no reason why walkers can't proceed at their natural pace and meet up for breaks at pleasant spots and at any path junctions where a mistake could be made. Some will want to stop frequently to take photographs or to adjust layers of clothing, while those who are less fit will need to stop frequently on steep bits. People not used to striding out may display a lack of natural rhythm; with time this will rectify itself but, meanwhile, don't let them get in front of you.

Then there is the issue of whether your interests and tastes are compatible. You might think that anyone who undertakes a long walk must have a certain level of interest in the outdoors, but nature means different things to different people. It helps if you aren't the only one pausing constantly to take photos or inspect flowers. You certainly can't assume that all walkers will be equally interested in other cultures. If you're walking in a country where living conditions and social habits differ greatly from your own, make sure your companions won't behave in a boorish fashion and give you a bad case of social agony. Money can also be a major point of friction among travelling companions. Fortunately, walkers don't get many opportunities to spend much of it, but you should ascertain that all parties are budgeting for the same type of accommodation and are prepared to endure the same level of privation.

Ideally, travelling companions should have some overlapping but also complementary skills so that each gains from the other. If I could choose the ideal group of companions, I might include a philosopher, a geologist, a botanist, a twitcher and a nurse.

CANINE COMPANY

Should you desire company on a walk, there is, of course, another option. While I have never personally walked with a dog, I have encountered them in some very hard-to-reach places. French people take small dogs on surprising routes, tucking them under one arm when the going gets tough. The British, too, are keen on canine company: we met a collie named Sadie who was taking her humans for a walk across England. Above Honister Pass, we encountered a beagle carrying a first aid kit; he was so excited to see us that he dropped his cargo.

These were mere walking dogs, but in the Pyrenees we met a black shaggy thing of indeterminate lineage, roped up for mountain climbing. There is a venerable history of climbing dogs. One alpine enthusiast, the Reverend Coolidge, was often accompanied by his aunt and his dog when climbing mountains during the 1860–80s. Tschingel the beagle climbed sixty-six major peaks, including eleven first ascents, and was fêted at a reception in Chamonix following her ascent of Mont Blanc. She was nominated as an honorary member of the Alpine Club but her gender—not her species—was something of an issue. Apparently she was an excellent guide over glaciers, being able to sniff out the cool air of concealed crevasses.

Myles Dunphy, a pioneer of bushwalking in Australia, also enjoyed the company of his dog on walks in the 1930s. Unlike Tschingel, who preferred to go unshod, Dextre Symbol was happy to wear leather doggy-boots when bushwalking. These days, this would be frowned upon (not the name—bizarre names are now *de rigueur* for both children and pets) as dogs can be a danger to native animals in the bush.

However, there are places where canine company is permitted, and if your dog shows enthusiasm for adventure, it may be worth investigating. There's no point trying to take a cat on a long walk. They are not team players and their lack of enthusiasm for the venture will only disappoint.

8. Kit and caboodle

. . . .

On a long walk, I find great joy in living simply, with minimal belongings and making only a limited use of technology. This is perhaps a little fanciful, considering the elaborate nature of modern walking clothes and gear, but everything is relative. It's liberating for those of us with too many possessions at home to get up each morning, look out the window and have what you see determine precisely what clothes you don.

Some people find it more difficult to give up luxuries. Frank Moorhouse, an Australian author who likes to go bush from time to time, states that he does not share 'the rigid functionalism of most backpacking practice—the principle that everything carried must have a practical use and be the lightest and smallest available'. He claims that 'On long trips I carry a few things which give me pleasure from their design and presence.' I do too,

Frank: very light and tiny, well-designed objects. In the words of French writer Antoine de Saint-Exupéry: 'He who would travel happily must travel light.'

One sure way to spoil a good walk is to carry too much. How much is too much? A book I looked through—clearly aimed at the novice walker—advised that 'experience will tell you how much you can carry, but aim for less than 25 kg (55 lb)'. It would take no more than thirty seconds of experience to tell me that I should aim for a great deal less than 25 kilograms. The author, although clean-shaven, is a former commando with, apparently, no concept that people smaller than he might not want to lug half their body weight around on their back. A more useful recommended maximum weight is no more than one-quarter of your own weight.

Innovative materials mean clothing and equipment are getting lighter and lighter, making the load easier to bear. Much of the weight consists of bits and bobs that you add for highly unlikely eventualities. After each trip I unpack, make a mental note of the items that I never used, and then inevitably pack them again the next time—along with a few extra things I won't need, just in case. The only thing I should repack that I hope never to use is the first aid kit.

What you take is determined by where you're walking and at what time of year: most obviously, warm clothing for a cold climate, and sun protection for a hot one. Specific items will vary for individuals, but I've included my checklist at the back of the book for the reader who seeks particulars. We sent this list, or one like it, to young nephew Jez before he joined us overseas, but he mistook it for a list of *necessary* rather than *sufficient* items. To it, he added numerous belongings, presumably using Frank Moorhouse's principles of selection. Among them were two long woollen scarves in the colours of his favourite football team, a heavy cotton jersey in the colours of the Australian rugby team and a weighty electric razor. I swear my facial hair grew faster than his.

Over time, you may well grow quite fond of your kit, but it's wise to be on good terms with it from the start. If there's anything in the pack that displeases you before you even leave home, replace it. Don't assume that you can buy necessary gear in the country where you will be walking: even if there are suitable outlets there, you may not have adequate opportunity to select items carefully. If you're joining a guided trek, you might be able to hire down jackets or other items for which you have no further use.

FANCY FOOTWEAR

In our family, coming of age was marked not with a licence to drive a car or to drink alcohol, but with a pair of leather walking boots, presented once it was certain that your feet had stopped growing. Mine were Diadoras, given to me amid great ceremony on my seventeenth birthday. They served me faithfully for many years until, in my late twenties, I was seduced by another Italian and ran off with a pair of Scarpas. This relationship flourished (apart from a short fling with a Chinese pair of synthetics) and I wore through several pairs. In Switzerland, however, my head was turned by a dashing pair of Lowes: they're light, they're Gore-Tex . . . and red! I delayed wearing them, spinning out the anticipation, but recently gave them their first outing on a four-day hike in the Australian Alps. We are very happy together and I break into a smile every time I swing a leg forward and catch sight of one.

Apart from colour, footwear should be appropriate for the terrain you expect to encounter. If you're planning to stay on well-graded paths, walking shoes will no doubt be sufficient. On rocky terrain, the ankle support a boot provides is essential. I often wear shoes on day-walks but on long excursions I always wear my boots. In wet and cold conditions, you'll want some that are waterproof. Modern boots are surprisingly lightweight and don't need the long period of 'breaking in' that older boots once did.

When buying boots, keep in mind that feet swell when walking on a warm day as opposed to standing around in an air-conditioned shop. Head to a retail outlet where the assistant will understand what level of activity you're intending. Some shops have a ramp that allows you to simulate walking downhill, which is when your toes will hurt if your shoes are too small or too wide. In the absence of a slope, tap your boot toe on the ground. Walk around the shop a lot. You should be able to wiggle your toes—but if you can wiggle the whole front section of your foot from side to side, the sole is too wide. The heel should feel snug. You may be allowed to trial them, indoors, at home and return them if necessary; if so, include plenty of stairs in your homework.

Some boots are entirely satisfactory apart from their laces. Lacings often need tightening after walking for an hour, but there is nothing more frustrating than having to stop frequently and tie yet another double bow. Replace laces that slip with a pair of reliable ones. Check the treatment for maintaining the material of the boots and then be diligent in its application: cracks and fissures let water in. Boots come with thin footbeds that can be removed to speed up drying. For added support and comfort, augment or replace these with a pair of footbeds bought separately.

For a long walk, you should take a spare pair of light but durable footwear to wear in the evenings, or in towns, or as substitutes if problems arise. What you take depends on your itinerary: reef sandals are fine for lolling around in warm climates and can be worn with socks (a good look!) if the evenings are cool. They are also excellent for river crossings. In cold climates, your spare footwear might be trainers or something passing for regular shoes.

Skimping on the cost of footwear is a big mistake for walkers. Before heading off to the Alps, we strongly recommended that co-walker Brett bought something that offered ankle support and had good tread. His purchase of the cheapest boots available from a budget chain store soon turned into a serious health risk. And not just to Brett's blistered feet: we had to put his shoes outside any shared room each night so as not to succumb to the fumes. They were binned well before the end of the trip.

THE RIGHT BACKPACK

You know a walk has been successful when you grow to love your pack. As Robert Louis Stevenson wrote in his essay 'Walking Tours', 'During the first day or so of any tour there are moments of bitterness, when the traveller feels more coldly towards his knapsack, when he is half in a mind to throw it bodily over the hedge . . .'. Fortunately, this relationship shifts: 'It becomes magnetic; the spirit of the journey enters into it.' And very soon, you adjust to each other's company, like old friends.

I'm very fond of my pack, which is adorned with the elevated title of 'Lady Pulsar' and, like the name, is well behind the times. She perches on my back at a jaunty angle that disturbs anyone walking behind me and haughtily resists any attempts by friends to adjust and straighten her. She has a pocket on each side that allows me to reach for a water flask without removing the pack. As a result she is a wide load and somewhat heavier than the svelte models of today, but she has much more character and I have no qualms about sitting on her when I want to rest, which is more than most friends will allow.

For a walking tour, a top-opening rucksack or backpack (rather than a 'travel pack') is essential. A zip at the base of the pack means you don't have to eject everything to reach the lower recesses. A few pockets are handy for storing things you need quickly, but don't get carried away or it'll be an elaborate treasure hunt every time you want to find your glasses. The capacity of a pack is measured in litres. Lady P is a modest 65 litres, larger than a day-pack but ideal for hut-to-hut walking. It can fit a half-share of camping gear in, but only just: I would have to strap gear on the outside for solo camping.

The other relevant measurement is a pack's height, and if you are particularly short or tall you need to have a pack fitted for the length of your torso. Jez's height necessitated a giant pack—and he made the mistake of filling it. In recent years, John has cunningly downsized to a 50-litre pack made of lightweight materials that is just adequate for hut-to-hut walking. Make sure there's space available for lunch supplies and for the clothes removed when you warm up.

Don't be rushed when purchasing a backpack. Packs on display are often stuffed with newspaper; turf this out and fill it with the sort of load you'll have to carry. When adjusted, the pack should sit comfortably on your hips. It should have tensioning straps (that run from the top of the pack to the shoulder straps) and perhaps a chest strap, but extra straps and gadgets are mere distractions. If you plan to drink from a hydration pack (discussed later), make sure there's a space for it.

Quite likely, you'll also need a day-pack. On long walks we stow a flimsy, fold-away type for day-walks *en route* and to use as hand luggage on a plane flight. If you're undertaking a walk where your luggage is transported for you, your day-pack must be more substantial and sturdy. (You should also seek advice from your trekking company regarding your main luggage, as a backpack may not be ideal.) A reliable day-pack is also preferable for a series of day-walks from a base. Like their larger counterparts, these have improved a lot recently: I prefer one that arches slightly off the back, with mesh to improve ventilation and absorb any sweat (or rather, 'glow').

WALKING CLOBBER

The American prophet of simple living, Henry David Thoreau, warned us to beware of all enterprises that require new clothes. Thoreau was a natural walker—it was his main means of travel—and he would have been puzzled by the idea of acquiring clothes specifically for the activity. Both he and his friend Ralph Waldo Emerson were quite right: simple clothes are all you need for walking. It's just that if you're walking any great distance, you'll want simple clothes that are also lightweight, quick-drying, and keep you cool or warm as required. I've encountered some stylish walkers on the track, but I'm aware that the same will never be said of me. For me, fashion is not an issue when choosing walking clothes (or any other clothes, as my friends will attest); comfort, temperature regulation and ease of laundering are.

There have been several developments in fabric production since Thoreau's days of leather and burlap, and even since my parents' days of moleskin and waxed cotton. A manual for the Sierra Club of outdoorsy Americans, published just thirty years ago, advises that jeans are fine for hiking but warns against wearing bell-bottoms. There are now fabrics that are feather-light and that draw up moisture, or 'wick' (from the Anglo-Saxon *weoce* for a reed), which is a good thing. Some even promise not to smell too much, which is definitely a good thing.

Two things are certain to change when you are walking: your skin temperature and the weather. You should be able to regulate your temperature by wearing clothes that can be easily adjusted, opening shirts or jackets at the neck, rolling up sleeves, unzipping vents. We swear by hiking trousers that have zips at mid-thigh level so that the lower section can be removed to create shorts. Ideally, the lower section fits over your boot so the change can be made in a matter of moments. I dislike any drag of fabric on the knees so I wear shorts whenever I can. When active, my body runs at a hot temperature (possibly because I'm rarely aerobically fit), so I also favour sleeveless tops with liberal applications of sunscreen. If you're prone to sunburn, long sleeves and covered legs are a sensible option.

In anything other than hot weather, you'll need to master the art of layering, particularly on the upper half of your body. The base layer should be fine wool or a synthetic with an antibacterial treatment. Cotton fails the wicking test and is to be avoided. In cold conditions, the base garment should be close-fitting to improve insulation, and you might consider thermal leggings as well as a thermal top. The mid layer should also be made of breathable and wicking fabric. Choose a shirt and shorts or trousers that allow for a full range of motion. When you stop for lunch or if there is windchill, add a fleece to this layer. Fleeces come in a range of weights and densities: a lightweight one is usually sufficient, especially when you're on the move. A full-length front zip also makes it easier to regulate your temperature. Finally, an outer layer or shell protects you from cold winds as well as rain and snow and I'll come back to this shortly. (I have to adjust layers frequently and have developed the ability to remove a fleece on the hoof, without taking off my pack. One day, I'll take a tumble midway through—it would really be better to pause for the task.)

The layering principle extends to the extremities. No matter what the temperature, I wear a short, thin, wicking sock under a thicker insulating sock. I've never been troubled by blisters, so this system appears to work; it certainly means that I can wash the liner socks in the evening and have them dry for the following day. You also need a spare, dry change of socks for evenings. For cold conditions, gloves are essential. If your circulation is compromised, consider wearing silk wicking gloves under waterproof, insulating ones. A lot of heat is lost from the head, so a hat with a wicking lining and a woollen outer maximises your chances of staying warm. For sun protection, you'll need a packable hat with a decent brim and a means of keeping it tight on your head in windy conditions.

For a week of walking, you'll need a change of clothes for the evening: a spare base layer and top, spare trousers, spare knickers and two pairs of outer socks. For a longer trip, I just add a top made of a different-weight fabric. To keep your load to a minimum, carry clothing that can be washed along the hike. Plan to regularly wash underwear, socks and shirts; the rest can wait. What you sleep in depends on whether you're a warm sleeper or not; I take a pair of old cotton shorts and a singlet that are reserved for sleepwear and replace them with thermals in cold conditions. Those who prefer to sleep naked may need to revisit this habit when sharing a room with strangers. If swimming is on the cards, take underwear that can do double-duty.

If you want to look really serious as a walker, wear gaiters. Not just those little ankle collars that prevent grit and snow falling into your boots, but ones that go right up to your knees and protect you from leaping snakes and gouging vegetation. I get far too hot and bothered in mine so I seldom pack them— I guess I'm just not that serious.

WATERPROOFING EVERYTHING
One of the stranger sights along the path is the poncho, a large sheet of nylon that covers both pack and walker. Quite aside

from appearance—do you want to scare small children?—these are no good in the wind or in driving rain. If you're walking in a cold climate, where the combination of cold and rain can be lethal, you'll need to get serious about keeping yourself and, more importantly, your spare clothing dry.

Luckily, we live in the age of Gore-Tex, a semi-permeable membrane that resists water but allows sweat to evaporate; it was originally developed as a spin-off from artificial kidney research. Patents on this fabric have lapsed and some other brands offer the same effect, so some waterproof jackets made of breathable fabrics are now more affordable. Seams, zips and pockets are the vulnerable points on a jacket, so it's worth looking closely at the quality of sealant tape used and considering whether the design encourages water to collect at such points. I like a jacket that is quite long, to keep my bottom reasonably dry, and with a peaked cap to keep rain out of my eyes. An internal chest pocket is useful for keeping your map or a small camera dry and handy.

Waterproof trousers are a boon if the weather is really grim. Make sure yours can be pulled over your boots (mine have ankle zips), otherwise it's too much trouble to don them on the path. For occasional use, these don't need to be made of fancy fabric; the lighter the better.

Backpacks are never entirely waterproof. On a long walk, we carry the means to waterproof them both inside and out: a sodden pack is really heavy, and wet contents can be a disaster. I heartily recommend lining your pack inside with a large, lightweight dry-sack (or a garbage bag) and then, when rain starts falling, whipping on a fold-away pack cover.

TREKKING POLES

More than a decade ago, I was diagnosed with arthritis in my knees. This was inevitable: as a child my knees used to click so loudly on bending that I was thrown out of public libraries. The doctor, on witnessing their knobbliness, cried, 'My god, how long have they looked like that?!' I went and bought a pair of trekking poles and kept on walking.

The use of a pole is nothing new. The renowned English lexicographer Samuel Johnson, who was a large bear of a fellow, relied on a walking stick—of English oak, studded with nails to mark off a foot and a yard measure—while travelling through Scotland. He was most aggrieved when it was lost, claiming it had surely been pinched, given the rarity of a piece of timber in the treeless north. And he had a point: you can't rely on picking up a suitable stick along the path for the tricky sections. Better to bring your own—and better still to bring two.

Today's trekking poles are lightweight, adjustable and compact, and they aren't only for walkers with dodgy knees. Apart from reducing the load on your knees and hips, they improve your balance on rough ground, in slippery conditions and when crossing streams. They are invaluable on long, steep descents. When buying a pair, make sure they collapse enough to fit into your pack, or strap neatly to the outside for travel or for when you need hands free for scrambling. Choose ones with a comfortable handle that won't get sweaty. Tungsten tips will outlast other metals. Extra money buys poles with shock absorption, which is helpful on hard surfaces such as roads but a waste of money and energy elsewhere. In general, adjust your poles to give you a ninety-degree angle at the elbow, lengthen them for descents and shorten them for steep slopes.

WATER VESSELS

Call me old-fashioned, but I still prefer drinking from a flask to sucking away on those hydration pack thingies. I gave up sucking when I was weaned. A hydration pack is a flexible, refillable bladder with a drinking hose that stows in your backpack, allowing you to drink, hands-free, at frequent intervals, without interrupting your walk. Still, I like to pause for a drink while looking around and I can reach my flask without dropping my pack. This also lets me check the level of my water supply, which I can't do if it is concealed in my backpack. The tubes of hydration packs can get gunked up with suspect growths and are difficult to clean. Nevertheless, many walkers wouldn't use anything else.

Flask-drinkers can choose from an abundance of materials, such as stable plastics like Nalgene which are lightweight and clear. Refilled PET bottles should be used only once; they deteriorate and are also easily crushed. I'm sticking with aluminium flasks made by Swiss company Sigg, which come in jewel colours and always make me feel cheerful (which is useful when my boots are muddy). I also carry a plastic bladder that folds flat when empty, in case I need to carry more than a litre of water at any stage. If you're planning to walk in mountainous terrain where you'll frequently encounter fresh water that is safe to drink, consider strapping a lightweight mug to the outside of your pack; it will save you having to lie at stream level to get your fill. I have numerous photos of John in scenic locations, stretched out in obeisance to the local water god.

BITS AND BOBS

Be wary of unnecessary miscellanea—items may look small but they rapidly accrete, cluttering up your pack and adding to the weight. Most hostels and refuges expect you to have your own towel: a small, quick-drying microfibre towel is ideal. You should also carry an inner sheet—silk ones are wonderfully lightweight and comfortable—with an attached or separate pillow case. If you are opting to camp, your kit is instantly going to swell to include a tent, a sleeping bag, a sleeping mat, a stove, eating utensils and food. This burden can be reduced if you have company and are prepared to share the tent and stove, but you'll still know you're carrying a full pack. A torch—preferably one you can wear on your head—is essential whether you're camping or staying in huts.

Paper is heavy so, as discussed earlier, trim your walking notes and even your maps. If the walk is challenging, you'll generally be too knackered at the end of the day to read, but you might want a book for a train journey or for when bad weather has forced a change of plan. Several writers do suggest that if you read a book on a walking tour, it will take on a strange significance. Robert Louis Stevenson said, 'It seems as if it were a book you had written yourself in a dream.' Choose a book that is pithily written or, if you must carry a larger tome, consider passing on the first half to a companion while you complete the tale. Canny walkers sometimes leave a trail of discarded pages in their wake.

Other paperwork includes sufficient local currency for food and accommodation and, if you're heading abroad, a passport and tickets. Copies of travel insurance and vital documents could be added to a companion's pack for safety. A small notebook and pencil are useful even if you're not planning to write a journal.

Keep toiletries to a minimum, with small containers of toothpaste, sunscreen, shampoo and moisturiser. Replace the lipstick with lip balm. For a long walk, make sure you have nail scissors to trim your toenails. Make up a simple first aid kit, referring to the packing list at the back of this book for minimum contents (an emergency blanket sounds weighty but isn't). Pack earplugs for those nights in a shared dorm. Pack tissues that can double as toilet paper or vice versa. Sunglasses are essential for protecting the eyes from the glare of sun and snow.

Keep your map dry in a map case or a resealable plastic bag. Unless your compass has a lanyard, throw in a bit of string for measuring the route. Wrap a length of tape just below the handle of your poles; it may not be needed but it will help you quickly identify your poles hanging among others in the vestibule of a hut. A pocket knife is essential for cutting up lunch supplies and you might consider a small airtight box for quarantining smelly cheese or safeguarding ripe fruit. A tiny repair kit and a few safety pins could come in handy. A universal sink plug certainly will. A lightweight travel umbrella might appear a strange inclusion, but it can be useful for shade, in light rain, or as an emergency toilet shelter when walking in exposed terrain. The idea brings new meaning to the motto 'be prepared'!

Then there are lots of optional gadgets. A mobile phone is only useful if you have arranged roaming facility and there is coverage. A pair of small binoculars will help you observe wildlife. A GPS or navigation device proves handy if you are heading into uncertain territory. Most walkers will carry a small camera and enthusiastic photographers will want to carry more; there are further musings on photography in the penultimate chapter. If you have any device that needs recharging, make sure you have an adaptor to suit local fittings. One thing you shouldn't bring is your full set of keys. Leave the house keys with a neighbour. Take the car key if you must, but remove all those other unidentified keys that have accumulated on the ring.

I was alarmed to read, in an American book on hiking solo, a lengthy debate about whether or not to pop a gun into your pack. However, it isn't a new idea. In the nineteenth century Robert Louis Stevenson thought it prudent to carry a gun on walks: he was obsessed by the idea that 'jocular persons' would discover his campsite and play practical jokes on him. A gun seems a somewhat humourless response.

PACKING AND HOISTING

Packing is a balancing act between access and comfort. A well-packed rucksack keeps the weight close to your back and between your hips and shoulders: this way, your centre of gravity is less compromised and you're more stable on tricky terrain. If you're camping, a stove, fuel, tent poles and food are the objects that you'll want to arrange midway, close to your back. If you're walking hut to hut you shouldn't have many heavy items, so just pack them in the centre, near your spine, with lightweight items up top. The whole thing should be balanced so you don't sway from side to side as you walk. Then there are things you'll want to find quickly along the way: sunglasses, hat and sunscreen (or, conversely, gloves and woolly hat), camera, map, rain jacket, water. The first aid kit doesn't need to be immediately to hand but you should know where to find it. If you have to attach anything to the outside of your pack, make sure it's lightweight and secure. Inside the pack, loose items should be grouped logically into what my mum used to call dillybags (and still does). My dictionary suggests 'dilly' is an Australian Aboriginal term; it's certainly got more character than 'stuff sack'.

With luck, your backpack isn't too heavy to lift; a hernia is never a good start to a walking holiday. If there is any doubt, bend your knees and lift the pack onto one thigh, slip one arm through the shoulder strap and then swing the pack onto your shoulder before putting on the other shoulder strap. Clasp the hip belt and the chest strap and adjust the tensioning straps. These should be adjusted from time to time as you walk, bringing the load closer to you on uphills and relaxing them on downhills. I also tighten the hip belt occasionally to stop the weight dragging on my shoulders.

PACKING FOR FLIGHT

A slight complication in your packing routine arises if your trip begins with a plane flight. For a start, you have to consider that your backpack may get lost in transit, taking a different world itinerary from you. Most often, misplaced luggage is located and delivered to you within a couple of days, but this can be disastrous if you planned to walk immediately on landing, as happened to us once. To circumvent this problem, friends Peter and Louise recently set off for a three-week walking holiday on the Continent with only day-packs so they could walk straight off the flight—admirable, but not something many of us could achieve. I always wear my boots onto the plane, knowing it would be difficult to replace them. (I usually take them off and put them in the overhead locker, much to others' disgust.) I also take my camera and any paperwork I've carefully assembled. What you can't take in your carry-on luggage is your penknife or scissors, so make sure such items are safely stowed in your main pack.

Backpacks can get damaged in transit. Reduce the risk of straps being torn by doing up all buckles and clasps and, if possible, placing the pack in a large, clear plastic bag that can be secured when you check it in. Some airlines can provide such bags at the counter. On a few occasions we've bound up our packs with shrink wrap that we happened to have handy and I've since noticed this service on offer in a few airports.

For a long plane journey we wear some items of clothing that are on their last legs but that won't quite get us arrested for vagrancy. That way, as soon as we've reached our first night's destination, we ditch the whiffy T-shirt, elastic-challenged underwear and holey socks and so postpone the inaugural clothes wash while instantly lightening our load.

Some items that have travelled well with you are hard to discard. I have a few items that keep making 'just one last trip': a battered drink flask that harbours who-knows-what bacteria, the cotton shorts that I have slept in for years. When the time comes for kit to be abandoned, think of it as a natural process, as Ralph Waldo Emerson did: 'When you have worn out your shoes, the strength of the shoe leather has passed into the fiber of your body. I measure your health by the number of shoes and hats and clothes you have worn out.'

With four pairs of walking boots reassigned as gardening boots, I must be looking pretty fit—a pity the garden doesn't.

9. *Sustenance*

......

One of the great pleasures of walking is the appetite it gives for eating. There's an incredible sense of wellbeing to be gained from obeying the natural rhythms of developing a real hunger and satisfying it, as opposed to eating at the appointed hour, whether hungry or not. On a long walk, eating is no longer a tired habit or an attempt to alleviate boredom; it's a welcome necessity. For those of us who have an otherwise small appetite, or who are wary of the bloating effects of overeating, a long walk blesses us with the capacity to eat more and removes any skerrick of guilt we might suffer in doing so. G.M. Trevelyan claimed this also extends to the consumption of liquids at the end of the day: 'And if you have walked twenty-five miles and are going on again afterwards, you can imbibe Falstaffian potions and still be as lithe and ready for the field as Prince Hal at Shrewsbury.' Sadly, there's no medical evidence that walking prevents hangovers.

What's more, far away from places where fast food is the norm, we can rediscover the pleasure of enjoying simple, real food. The countryside is still the providore of very fresh vegetables, daily-baked bread and remarkable cheeses. The fare may not be sophisticated but it will revive the most jaded palate. Even more so for the walker: after a day on the path, everything tastes that much better. One of the most memorable dishes I've ever consumed was after a very long day spent descending from the Maritime Alps in southern France. We arrived late, unexpected and bone-weary at a *gîte d'étape* near the perched village of Saorge and were received with much grace and a large bowl of butter beans, fresh picked from the garden, served warm and dressed to perfection. Other dishes followed, but that one made us feel that all was right with the world.

The civilising aspect of sharing a meal still applies. The breakfast table is an ideal forum to preview the route for the day. Along the path, walkers inevitably cluster at a good viewpoint to eat, and such breaks afford a good opportunity to talk to others you've just met, all the while basking in the sun or sheltering from a stiff breeze. After the day's walk, there's nothing quite like sitting around a table and sharing a soup tureen with appreciative eaters. Fortunately, servings at establishments for walkers are usually generous. On an organised trek in less developed countries, you'll find the food plentiful but perhaps limited in range. Keep in mind that the cook's family probably hasn't seen this much meat in their lifetime.

On any long walk, you'll need to carry some food. The art, of course, is to carry enough but not too much. It's important, when on an expedition, not to be tempted like A.A. Milne's Christopher Robin, who announced quite early on 'that we ought to eat all our Provisions now, so that we shan't have so much to carry'. Keep some emergency rations in your pack; if you finish the walk and eat them on the bus home, then you've catered well.

DRINKING WATER

The other important matter is What to Drink. Slothing around at home, I rarely drink water, consuming more in the way of coffee, tea and alcoholic beverages. On the track, however, my body tells me what it needs and that is always water. Even if I'm not raising a noticeable sweat, my water flask is a dear friend. Filling it is the tricky part. I like to have a litre of water on hand but in warm weather, or if water is likely to be scarce, I carry extra in a clear plastic bladder. If you do run short of water, there is no physiological argument for rationing it. Drinking as your thirst requires will postpone dehydration and, with luck, you will reach a water source before you die.

To avoid such a predicament, read any track notes in advance to assess how readily available water is likely to be, and always carry extra water if in doubt. The harsh reality is that each litre of water weighs a kilogram, and you will need to drink more on warm days and at altitude. The one occasion when we've been seriously low on water was across a dry section of Corsica. The temperature was in the thirties, the streams marked on the map were all dry and we were walking up and down a lot of hills. We detoured a short way to a high village, but there was no shop or bar or obvious water fountain. By an open door, I made enquiries of a man who was preserving bits of a wild boar he had recently shot, and he insisted I fill our flasks with spring water that he had chilled. I've never met a nicer hunter.

Assuming you find water, you'll need to ensure that it's potable. Giardia, an intestinal parasite found in the gut of warm-blooded animals and transmitted to water, can cause all kinds of nasty gastric problems. I've read that most wilderness water in North America contains a form of giardia and another nasty protozoan, cryptosporidium. Upstream grazing, human settlement, even just a camping site used by careless people can all contaminate a stream. Don't rely on water colour as an indicator of health, as clear water can be affected. Conversely, in Australia we often encounter unpolluted streams tinted brown by the tannin in shrubs. Be careful but not paranoid: I've never been made ill despite a lot of stream-sipping. If you need to drink suspect water, you can rid it of dangerous impurities by bringing it to a rolling boil, by adding iodine or water-purifying tablets, or by pouring it through a fine, giardia-rated filter. We carry tablets.

On occasion, the water supply at a hut below a glacier might be labelled not potable; this is more likely due to its mineral composition rather than giardia. At one such hut we ungenerously suspected our hosts of profiteering, until we were freely presented with a litre of bottled water each at dinner.

If, like Hilaire Belloc, you consider water to be 'the mere beverage of the beast', you could carry an additive to change the flavour. For years we carried a vial of lurid green powder with us on the path, but it rattled untested around the bottom of the pack. (By all means carry sachets of rehydration powder to replace salts in case of dehydration.) If you're carrying a stove, a brew-up at lunchtime is a possibility, but despite the pleasure I derive from a cup of tea or coffee, it's an awful lot of faffing about. I suspect Belloc, who walked great distances, was more in favour of an alcoholic beverage. Wine is poor value for its weight; a flask of something more potent such as brandy or cognac will serve better. Obviously, significant quantities should not be consumed along the path, especially in cold temperatures or at altitude, as alcohol can depress breathing and cause dehydration and frostbite. However, a celebratory nip won't do too much harm. Our French friend Paul can be relied on to produce the *pastis* on momentous occasions, and a little goes a long way as water is added before quaffing.

PROVISIONING

No matter whether you're self-catering or just need food for the middle of the day, you have an excellent excuse to go shopping. I'm not a natural shopper, but provisioning is a different matter. If you're in a foreign country, there may be markets to explore or specialist shops to enter. France is slowly succumbing to the hypermarket on the edge of town, but in much of the countryside there is still a culture of the specialist shop—boulangerie, épicerie, pâtisserie, charcuterie—and each one needs to be investigated for proper provisioning. If you can visit an open market, the experience is even more invigorating and a great opportunity to see the locals in action.

Allow time to shop for food in the town where you are spending the night before heading off on your walk. Ascertain when you will get the chance to resupply, and note local opening hours. In many regions, shops close for a couple of hours in the middle of the day so shopkeepers can enjoy a long lunch or a siesta. Markets tend to be a morning-only affair. Also, don't assume every hamlet will have a shop. We once ran out of supplies in the Dordogne and had to wait for the travelling grocer's van to arrive in a village: the street was empty one moment, then buzzing with smocked housekeepers the next.

Most likely, you need to stock up on provisions for a picnic lunch. If the itinerary doesn't allow fresh bread each day, look for wholemeal or rye bread that keeps longer. Beyond a couple of days, crackers are a better option. To accompany it, you might buy cured sausage or meat and firm local cheeses. If you're in pâté or terrine territory, even better, but buy modest portions, as these won't keep well. We always buy some fresh fruit, preferably something we can't get at home—but pack any fruit with care. We discovered the hard way that ripe persimmons don't travel well, and in Chamonix I opened my pack (in which John had secreted a punnet of strawberries) to find that my entire wardrobe would be a fetching pink for the rest of the journey. Carry a lidded plastic lunch box for items that may morph, melt or exude a strong perfume. (We also know from experience that the aroma of pungent cheese can otherwise permeate a backpack for many weeks!)

If you are camping and need to purchase all your supplies, you need food that is lightweight and nourishing. You will need to visit a supermarket for an array of dried and semi-dried foodstuffs such as muesli (or granola), powered milk, instant soups, noodles, lentils, instant pasta or rice meals, flavoured instant couscous, cured meats, hard cheeses, foil sachets of tuna, crackers and small packets of spread. In some countries, your choice will be limited and you might want to bring lightweight supplies from home, especially treats such as snack bars. If you can locate an outdoor sports shop, buy packets of freeze-dried meals that just require boiling water: they are incredibly light and simple to prepare and are vaguely like the meals they purport to have once been. Some brands have a wide range of flavours, which is just as well if you're on a long hike. I've even seen a freeze-dried strawberries-and-ice-cream dessert. My recommendation is to keep your cuisine simple: any food will taste wonderful if you're hungry enough.

Everyone, self-sufficient or catered to, will need something to munch on the track. Traditionally, this has been a mix of nuts and dried fruit, referred to by serious walkers as 'scroggin' or, in North America, 'gorp'. Magazines aimed at outdoor enthusiasts inform me that there are now various hugely expensive high-energy bars available that will boost my performance. My question to old and new alike is, why bother when you can eat chocolate? (Admittedly, friends recently introduced me to a very palatable scroggin that contained dried apple and apricot, pumpkin seeds, pecans and plenty of chocolate bits.) John always likes to buy a little something from the pâtisserie. It doesn't matter what it weighs—it always gets eaten fairly early, à la Christopher Robin.

WILD FOOD

Another way of keeping your energy levels up is by eating wild food that you discover along the path. The woods in Europe are dotted with little old men and women picking wild mushrooms. We've studied the charts on display in the windows of chemists (one of the duties of the French *pharmacien* is to confirm if the fungi you've picked are edible) and there appears to be very little difference between some rated *comestible* and those marked with a skull and crossbones. Not wanting to invite death, we've never picked our own, though we once had some huge cèpes forced on us by a couple we encountered, who insisted that we pass them on to the chef of wherever we were staying. The cèpes reappeared on our plate at dinner that night, lightly sautéed and fragrantly seasoned. If you can master the charts, you'll do very well.

Often I've been chatting to John, explaining a theory or two, and turned to find him detained by a blackberry vine or a mulberry tree. He is an incorrigible gleaner, helping himself to any fruit or nuts that the farmer may have overlooked or that are in the public domain.

I'm not certain that the rules of gleaning extend to sampling grapes from vines that have yet to be harvested. John insists that it's akin to sampling the first pressing. In Chianti, where he sampled quite a few, we decided to celebrate an excellent day's walking by enjoying a *rosso* from a particular vineyard we'd become lost in earlier that day. There were several on the restaurant's wine list and, having chosen the inexpensive one, we were a little concerned when a trolley appeared and the waiter conducted an elaborate decanting routine, then poured the wine into really big glasses. No one else in the dining room had really big glasses or a trolley and everyone had paused to watch the show. Fearing we had accidentally misordered, we spent the evening worrying whether the wine tasted modest or like the €150 one we saw listed below. At the meal's end we asked for our *conto* and were relieved to discover that any reserve wines—even the modest ones—get the trolley treatment. Sorry, that doesn't have much to do with wild food. But it was an unexpected gustatory adventure, all the same!

THE DIURNAL DIET

How often you need to eat will vary from walker to walker. We have a couple of active friends with whom we don't attempt to cover much ground: a day walking with Lani and Mike is heavily punctuated with either food stops or their inevitable consequence. That's the prerogative of vegetarians, apparently.

Some people can persist without food longer than others. I have sufficient reserves of fat in my upper thighs (the evolutionary triumph of the pear-shaped body) to see me a long way without a meal. John, on the other hand, is never keen to forgo lunch simply because of a snowstorm, and I have been forced to walk in circles to keep warm while he studiously prepares himself an elaborate something. Having said that, it is important to keep energy levels up to the task and worth noting that at high altitude appetite can be suppressed, so on these hikes you should carry particularly tempting foodstuffs.

Breakfast

Mark Twain said 'nothing helps scenery like bacon and eggs', and if you stay at a British B&B, you'll undoubtedly discover whether he was right. We find that breakfast in such establishments, where you're also served an array of numerous other fried goods, sets us up for the day and we can forgo further food until afternoon tea. In sharp contrast, breakfast in a European mountain hut will probably consist of slightly stale bread and jam—but at least there's good coffee. Those walking hut to hut may purloin any leftover bread for their lunch, but this should be done discreetly, as lunch supplies are often available at a cost.

Luncheon

Getting a meal during the day can be a challenge for walkers. A couple of my friends solved it by munching through an enormous block of chocolate each day as they walked the outback Larapinta Trail. I'm the last one to refuse chocolate, but even I would hesitate at that. We prefer to have a brief but civilised picnic lunch, enjoying some of the provisions mentioned earlier and giving a boost to body and spirit on a demanding day. Our friend Gigi can be relied upon to revive flagging morale by pulling the most surprising delicacies from her voluminous pack and sharing them around.

Choose your lunch spot carefully, waiting until the view is worthy and the conditions are good (sheltered from wind or sun, for example). Water in motion (a gurgling stream, crashing waves, a breeze-kissed tarn, a waterfall falling) gives you something pleasant to look at; even a glacier, slow though it may be, can be watched for the thrill of seeing an icefall. A notable feature or landmark makes the break more memorable. Unfortunately, mountain tops or passes are often too blustery for comfortable dining, but you can usually find a good spot a short way below on the more sheltered side. If the weather is really foul, just take what you can get. We have broken into the occasional empty cowshed to eat something during wild weather. These are surprisingly comforting places, as many cows would no doubt attest, but not as comfortable as a pub or mountain refuge for a light lunch. I say 'light' because to this day John has never quite recovered from the huge mound of *alpler maccheroni* that he consumed in an Austrian *berghaus* one lunch time. It was immediately followed by a steep incline at which, it must be told, he baulked. Tempting though the menu may be, go for the soup.

Have to hand some food that can be eaten easily so that, if bad weather and lack of shelter should make a sit-down lunch impossible, you can at least eat something while walking. Robert Louis Stevenson, caught out in rain, had to resort to a supper of Bologna sausage and chocolate: 'It may sound offensive, but I ate them together, bite by bite, by way of bread and meat.' He's quite right, it does sound offensive—but it doesn't compete with the culinary desperation of Douglas Mawson, who had to eat his huskies when his Antarctic expedition went awry: '29 December . . . Had a great breakfast off Ginger's skull—thyroid and brains.'

The evening meal
William Hazlitt, who didn't condone talking while walking, did admit: 'I grant, there is one subject on which it is pleasant to talk

on a journey; and that is, what one shall have for supper when we get to our inn at night.' I find this topic usually surfaces about an hour after lunch. On a walking excursion, dinner becomes something rather special. As G.M. Trevelyan wrote: 'After a day's walk, everything has twice its usual value. Food and drink become subjects for epic celebration, worthy of the treatment Homer gave them. Greed is sanctified by hunger and health.' The evening meal is the walker's just reward.

If you're overnighting in a village or town, you'll possibly have a choice as to where and what you eat. One of John's simple pleasures is to stroll up and down the street, considering his dining options. If there is limited choice, he might be a little glum; if it's closing day and there is no dining, I'm facing a very bleak evening. A picnic of cold scraps on your bed is not a satisfactory solution to a walker's hunger. In youth hostels and in some huts you can prepare yourself a hot meal; this is an option in most French refuges, and a necessity in New Zealand huts. It's interesting to watch the various approaches taken to hut cooking: I've seen young hikers produce manifold tins of ingredients and empty them into a huge pot; elsewhere we've met two aspiring actors who nibbled on stale bread rolls and hungrily eyed our meals. They were probably too young to have seen *Withnail and I*.

The best option, to my mind, is the evening meal that is prepared and served by someone else in the establishment where you will be sleeping. Half-board in a village or town hotel is generally a wonderful thing but there is an inverse relation between the popularity of the destination and the quality of the fixed meal. Our best dining experience was at a modest *pensione* in Campo di Giove in the Italian Maiella mountains, not a place overrun by tourists. For four nights, the mother of the house cooked us up a storm of five-course dinners replete with tender slow-braised lamb, meatballs with crepes, plus side dishes of stuffed mushrooms and other vegetables given individual treatment. The fact that we were her only guests didn't interfere at all with our hostess's *bella cucina*.

In walkers' huts in Europe, the evening meal will be a much more simple but hearty repast of three courses—often vegetable soup, perhaps a stew with rice or noodles, and possibly tinned fruit or flan. Publisher George Routledge advised in 1875 that 'It is never wise to partake of any dish without knowing of what ingredients it is composed. You can always ask the servant who hands it to you.' Heeding this advice we did query the contents of one unidentified casserole and were cheerfully informed by the hut guardian that it was 'charmotte'; I spent some minutes dredging through my meagre French vocab to realise the joke. At least I hope it was a joke: both *le chamois* and *la marmotte* are protected in national parks. As the fixed meal does often feature local specialities, there is a danger that the same regional dish could appear repeatedly as you walk from hut to hut. Fortunately, this doesn't often happen. We walked for a month in Switzerland— which has a limited cuisine—and managed to get the same dish only twice. My strictly carnivorous companions were particularly anxious about revisiting *raclette*, a dish wherein large slabs of grilled cheese are delivered to your plate to be eaten with potatoes and gherkins.

Walkers with restricted diets face a problem in huts. High in the mountains, fresh vegetables are an unknown and you are unlikely to be served anything green. Huts serving fixed meals are getting better at offering a vegetarian alternative, but it is most often a scaled-down version of everyone else's plate. Where it's an option you should consider self-catering so that you get a more balanced meal. Fussy eaters will soon be sorted out by necessity.

A little after-dinner something
According to Robert Louis Stevenson, dinner is good,

> But it is at night, and after dinner, that the best hour comes. There are no such pipes to be smoked as those that follow a good day's march; the flavour of the tobacco is a thing to be remembered, it is so dry and aromatic, so full and so fine. If you wind up the evening with grog, you will own there was never such grog; at every sip a jocund tranquillity spreads about your limbs, and sits easily in your heart.

I can't vouch for the tobacco, not being a smoker (and it's no coincidence that these days few enthusiastic walkers are). I will confirm, though, that the finest digestive I've ever tasted followed a strenuous circuit up to La Brèche de Roland, a giant's bite out of the high mountain ridge that constitutes the Pyrenees. We'd approached the breach via an airy clamber up the walls of the Cirque de Gavarnie that I can only describe as bowel-loosening. Halfway up, while encouraging John off a dizzy ledge, I spotted a wooden cross in memory of someone who had plummeted the previous summer. I didn't mention this until we were both safely in a bar back in Gavarnie, toasting our success with a pair of British journalists who had also survived the ascent. This is why cognac was invented.

10. Seeking shelter

......

'Thou art the thing itself; unaccommodated man is no more but such a poor, bare, forked animal as thou art.' Perceptive old Shakespeare knew that a sunny day in the Forest of Arden is one thing, but a night on King Lear's heath, exposed to the elements and without the comforts of civilisation, is quite another. The difference between a day-walk and an extended walking excursion is that in the latter you must find somewhere to lay your head at night. You will, most likely, need extra sleep on a long walk—nine hours a night or more—and how well you sleep will determine your fitness for walking the next day, so your choice of shelter is an important one.

Robert Louis Stevenson was determined to carry gear for camping on his Cévennes excursion, 'for there is nothing more harassing to an easy mind than the necessity of reaching shelter by dusk, and the hospitality of a village inn is not always to be reckoned sure by those who trudge on foot'. Sleeping out was, however, his option of last resort (travel writer Bruce Chatwin always considered Stevenson a fraud). When Ralph Waldo Emerson paid a visit to Yosemite in 1871, naturalist John Muir was bitterly disappointed that he could not convince the sage to camp out with him overnight. Emerson, at the age of 68, felt he had earned a decent bed.

Finding a decent bed, or any bed at all, can be tricky along some routes. In the era before the internet it was even more difficult. Luckily, hosts with beds on offer have always been keen to fill them. Before the Cinque Terre path drew crowds, we dropped down from the path to the fishing village of Vernazza and were grabbed by a tiny old woman garbed in black who dragged us to her guestroom above a boatshed hung with *sciacchetrá* grapes. These days she probably has her own website. Before you start to hunt, find out the local words for small inns or spare rooms. The list of websites at the back of the book will give you a starting point for a search. If you're not connected to the internet, the local tourist office can usually supply accommodation lists by post; ask specifically for simple accommodation in villages and the countryside.

If lodging is scarce and competition is likely, you might want to reserve a bed. We have tended not to book ahead, but have on occasion had to walk further than planned or spend more money than we would have liked, causing pain in foot or pocket accordingly. Where there is a choice, our decision is largely based on price. We go very low, working on the assumption we'll be tired enough to sleep wherever there's a mattress, a pillow and a blanket. This rule doesn't apply in cities, where a bargain can literally mean a basement or fleapit or brothel, but in rural areas 'cheap' generally equates to small and unadorned, family-run, and possibly even quaint. We have only once declined beds in an inn that proved *too* quaint: the attic dorm had to be accessed by ladder and was deficient in headroom. It was also crowded and its only happy occupant was, in fact, a dwarf.

SIMPLE SHELTERS

In harsh weather, shelter is also invaluable during the day for food and rest breaks. This may be as simple as a boulder or a stone wall that protects you from a chilly wind or blazing sun. On high, open ground, giant cairns can save the day. We've been known to 'let ourselves in' to quite a few herder's huts and barns so as to eat a hasty lunch or to put on warmer clothing and raingear. Rock overhangs that keep the rain from turning your lunch into mush are also welcome, but in the event of thunderstorms stay clear of shallow caves as they attract lightning. Deeper overhangs or caves afford better shelter. In New Zealand these are known as rock bivvies, one of which, at a hundred metres long, is known as the Ballroom. (John once spent several nights in an overhang in our local Budawang Mountains when the tent he thought he had packed turned out to be a beach shade.) Henry Russell, a nineteenth-century eccentric, lacked such natural shelters in the Pyrenees and so carved out several caves high on the flanks of Vignemale. He spent whole seasons up there, even holding formal dinners for friends who came to visit. When I ducked my head into one of these chambers, it looked poky (he can't have had many friends) and more than a little dank—but it certainly had atmosphere.

A tent can be an unnecessary burden. In Morocco, a lack of insects and mild temperatures make it possible to sleep under the stars, though a desert tent is handy if the wind picks up. Along the Bibbulmun Track in Western Australia, a series of roofed, three-sided shelters allows hikers to sleep outdoors and stay dry. Hardy types assured of such a sheltering structure might be content with a bivvy bag or mere sleeping bag. Others put their trust in a cover that can be strung up between trees—a tarp or a fly—to keep off light rain and dew. This is all very well in warm, dry climates; anywhere else and a tent is a sounder option. I have already admitted a healthy ambivalence to tents—our lightweight 'two-man' tent induces claustrophobia after two nights. Tents provided on a commercial trek should give you a bit more breathing space and keep you safer from the elements. Many treks also provide a tented dining area and a toilet tent, making it more like nomadic living than camping as we know it.

WALKERS' HUTS

Where walking is a popular undertaking, a basic form of accommodation can often be found. This can range in sophistication from an empty stone structure to a comfortable lodge staffed by someone who wants to feed you. The cost generally rises accordingly. Some, such as remote Scottish bothies or alpine bivouacs, are only intended for overnight or emergency use and are free, but walkers need to bring their own cooking equipment and sleeping bag.

New Zealand has a wonderful system of over 950 'backcountry' huts graded for facilities. Those on routes designated as Great Walks have all the essentials a walker needs, save food and a sleeping bag. Huts in other categories may also require you to carry your own stove, lighting, or sleeping mat; tariffs vary accordingly. The Department of Conservation in charge of the hut system has a website that provides details of each hut, including opening periods. Whether or not there is a resident warden, walkers must prepare their own meals.

France has an excellent form of lodging known as the *gîte d'étape*. These establishments are intended for walkers and horse-riders and are often found along the major footpaths. In instances where they are operated by the local community they will be spartan affairs, perhaps located in an old school or historic building, where you can cook your own meals. Most, though, are privately owned and more comfortable, with the owner on hand to provide a hearty dinner and breakfast. Sometimes, the *gîte* is simply one room of a small hotel, with dormitory bunks. Guests bring their own sleeping sheet or bag; the rest of the bedding is provided.

More ascetic—and reasonably so, considering the point of the exercise—are the Spanish *albergues* for pilgrims on the path to Santiago de Compostela. If you are woken at 4 a.m. for Matins, the first Catholic liturgy for the day, you have only yourself to blame.

MOUNTAIN REFUGES

Mountain areas in which there is a tradition of walking or climbing often feature refuges, a gift to walkers who seek a modicum of comfort. These may be owned by national mountain clubs (but allow non-members at a higher charge), operated by government agencies (commonly in national parks), or privately owned and run. European-style *refugios* are open during the summer in Patagonian national parks. Those ascending Kilimanjaro, nearby Mount Meru or Mount Kenya in Africa can lodge in huts during the strenuous climb. Traditional tea-houses in Nepal have dormitory arrangements that can be crowded, noisy and smoky; unless the weather is bad you might prefer to take the camping option. A series of lodges managed by the local community has just been built in the Annapurna Sanctuary to open up new routes for trekkers. There are also huts and refuges along many of the distance paths in South Africa.

A bed and meal in a refuge should ideally be booked ahead but latecomers are rarely turned away; there's always some space to sleep on the floor. Tariffs, which are reasonable when you consider the difficulty of supplying these locations, are usually payable only in local currency; don't rely on electronic credit services. What facilities can you expect? First, many have wonderful views and a terrace for enjoying them. Next, most have a vestibule for removing boots and leaving poles and possibly wet gear, although some also have a dedicated room near the generator where wet garments can be hung to dry. In the porch you will usually encounter shelves of slippers or clogs; no boots may be worn indoors. This practice has, I think, a delightfully levelling effect: hiking one-upmanship is practically impossible when you're all wearing slippers. Also provided are mattresses, blankets and pillows. Some refuges supply bed linen, but more often you will use your own sleeping sheet with an attached or separate pillow case.

On arrival, once my bunk has been secured, my priorities are:

- celebrating with a drink (especially if there is a view to be enjoyed)
- getting vaguely clean
- sorting out any wet or dirty gear
- making up a bed (this includes searching out my torch and earplugs)
- taking a book, maps or a notepad down to the communal area with the real intent of being sociable before dinner.

Water is sometimes in limited supply and a hot shower may incur a small extra charge, assuming there is hot water. Toilets, washrooms and dorms are unisex, but after a few days on the path everyone starts to look sexless, or at least of indeterminate gender.

There is a general lack of privacy that some might find disconcerting. In some huts you might score a small room with four or six bunks. Others feature large dormitories lined with long sleeping platforms and, if the refuge is busy, you get to wake up face to face with a total stranger, an experience you should only have in extreme youth. Avoid sharing a room with mountain climbers (these are the ones going to bed fully clothed) as they will inevitably be rising just as you start your first phase of rapid-eye-movement sleep. If the electricity comes from a generator it's usually turned off at 10 p.m., so to read beyond that hour you'll need your torch. Guests are expected to be quiet from that time until 6 a.m. or so. This, sadly, does not exclude snoring. Unless you are a brazen hussy or a cockalorum, you will have to forgo sex while staying in dorm accommodation. You'll probably be too weary anyway.

It's not all grim privation: there are some genuine pleasures in the communal life, including the chance to compare adventures and gain useful information about the next day's walk. The guardians of public huts are often enthusiasts and have chosen to fulfil this role for a limited period; they may even be mountain guides or ex-guides. Our host at the Cabane de Moiry, midway on the Walkers' Haute Route, even had a nearby pinnacle named after him. In such cases, your host can be a rich source of advice on path options, interpreting weather forecasts, and other useful matters. Despite having to budget for food, the cook always appears delighted if you ask for seconds (or fourths, in the case of our nephew Jez). There are always exceptions: we encountered a particularly surly warden high on the GR20 in Corsica. We should have foreseen this on approach, as his hut was flying a pro-independence flag featuring the silhouette of a man holding a machine gun. Despite an unseasonable blizzard and a hut filled with soaked refugee-campers, he refused to light the fire because it was the last night of the season and he'd already cleaned out the ashes. No one pressed the separatist too hard on the issue.

The owners of private huts can be charming or otherwise. Several times we've had luridly coloured liqueurs pressed on us *gratis* after dinner but such hosts are, on the whole, aware of being in business. There is one refuge on the Tour of Mont Blanc (TMB) with a notoriously poor welcome; even the official TMB website warns 'Accueil: médiocre'.

Most refuges can supply lunch and other daytime refreshment; indeed, day-walkers form much of their business. It's polite if not obligatory to buy something if you wish to rest on a refuge's terrace or to shelter indoors during the day. High mountain refuges are open for business only during the summer months, although some also open in winter for skiers. Most have a room or an out-building accessible all year round by walkers in need of emergency shelter.

HOSTELS

In the countryside, youth hostels these days are a bit of a misnomer; youth seldom seems to venture beyond the cities and so you're more likely to share a rural hostel with the middle-aged or active-but-downright-elderly. Hostels run by national associations are in decline, but increasing numbers of private hostels are cropping up. Both types range markedly in sophistication. Black Sail is a remote old shepherd's croft high in the English Lake District offering surprisingly good food in primitive conditions. Our hostel in Hohnstein, in Germany's Sächsische Schweiz national park, was a fourteenth-century fortress; it took us five hours to find the banqueting hall from our chamber in the west wing. In fact, hostels are often in quaint buildings: we have bunked in converted churches, a former Benedictine monastery and the station building on the railway platform of the Bridge of Orchy, along the West Highland Way.

Many hostels now offer rooms for couples or small groups, in addition to less expensive bunkrooms. British, Australian and Japanese youth hostels still separate the sexes in dorms, but this nicety doesn't always apply in Europe. This troubles few people today, whereas Robert Louis Stevenson was quite shocked to find himself in a room with a cooper, his wife and child all sharing the other bed. 'This was my first experience of the sort; and if I am always to feel equally silly and extraneous, I pray to God it be my last as well.' Fortunately, the human character is surprisingly adaptable, although I do wish German men wouldn't waltz around a dorm so starkly naked.

Britain also has a category of hostel known as a 'camping barn'; these are usually a converted farm building with basic facilities, but they're well priced and often well located for walkers. In Switzerland we've had a legitimate night's lodging in a cow barn, the cows busy grazing up on the *alpe*. (The earwigs, though plentiful, proved innocuous enough.) Sleeping on straw is not without literary precedent. Samuel Johnson, touring Scotland with his friend James Boswell in 1773, found the beds at one inn fell below his standards. He called for a bundle of hay to be brought into his room and slept upon it in his riding coat. Boswell, 'being more delicate', covered his own hay with sheets. I wonder if, like us, they pulled straws from their clothing for the rest of the journey.

B&BS

The very British institution of B&Bs is another blessing for walkers, as there is usually one in the smallest of villages and others dotted around the open countryside. As a guest you are essentially using someone's spare room and are often welcomed with a cup of tea and a little something (like a buttered teacake) on arrival. Some hostesses are a tad too houseproud, so watch those muddy boots. Some are downright obsessive; on leaving a B&B where our room had been pasted with stickers telling us what not to do, I felt compelled to advise Doris to get a life.

These home stays can be particularly enlightening in the countryside. We have overnighted in various farmhouses where John can keep a close eye on lambs; at one in Shropshire we even helped out with a lambing. It was a tricky procedure: a sheep was giving birth to a single lamb and the farmer wanted this mother to adopt a triplet from another ewe (since they can only suckle two). To achieve this, the farmer douses the 'orphan' with the fresh afterbirth to confuse the sheep. It was all pretty exciting, except that John was handed the newborn lamb to nurse while I had to mind the steaming placenta.

As you would expect, breakfast (and what a breakfast) is included in the tariff. Dinners are sometimes offered with advance notice. It can be a little awkward dining with your hosts (one spry widow tried chatting up my father in my presence) and a little quiet not dining with them. This use of the spare room is by no means a phenomenon restricted to the United Kingdom. Italy has also adoped the name B&B, while Germany, Austria and Switzerland have their *zimmer frei*. In France (where they are called *chambres d'hôte*), Australia and America, B&Bs are priced somewhat higher and are generally more upmarket. In Japan, the closest equivalent is *minshuku*, which offer your best chance to see Japanese daily life.

INNS AND OTHER OPTIONS

In larger villages and towns you'll have greater choice, but for character, colour and perhaps even charm, make a point of staying in small, family-owned hotels. These go by a variety of names, but *pension* will work in most European countries—and they are even making an appearance in Japan, where they cater for outdoorsy types. Japan also has traditional inns known as *ryokan* where, as in refuges, you exchange your boots for slippers. As a point of difference, you sleep on a futon on a tatami floor.

Small hotels or inns tend to be much more personal. In Wales I was the lone guest at the Half Moon Hotel in Llanthony in the shadow of the Black Mountain. The owner, a man years ahead of others in terms of energy efficiency, supplied me with a small bar-heater that followed me from living room to dining room to bedroom. When there are other guests, you may get to know them quite well as you compete for use of the bathroom down the corridor.

There are, of course, all kinds of lodging to be had. One of the strangest we've experienced was in Le Châble in Switzerland where we had the sole use of the town avalanche shelter, a windowless bunker tucked into the hillside, with airlocks, emergency stores and a surreal, end-of-the-world atmosphere. Should your lodging be not quite to your liking, you have the advantage that, as a wayfarer, you won't be there for very long.

11. Finding the way

......

Just because you plan to walk on a path, this does not excuse you from having a fair idea of where you are at any one time. Basic navigation skills are really useful for knowing (a) where on the path you probably are and (b) whether you're still on the path at all.

On high, open fells the mist can descend with surprising speed, rendering a route far from obvious. Landslips or fire can erase all signs of a path. Even in the perfectly waymarked Vanoise Alps in France, our friend Sue—walking apart from her companion after bickering—managed to divert onto a minor footpath and scale a small peak before realising her error. A mountain rescue helicopter was involved and the pilot was perfectly charming about the whole affair. Sue's problem stemmed from the fact that she was not in command of the map: that is, she wouldn't have been able to read it even if she'd had it in her possession.

Robert Louis Stevenson was in possession of both map and compass while crossing the Cévennes, but he often chose to seek direction from the natives, many of whom found his manner pompous and took pleasure in leading him astray. If you can muster less pomp, asking directions can be a good way of meeting people, if not of finding the way. Quite possibly you have a guidebook with a sketch map, or perhaps even a personal guide, and there's no great imperative for you to navigate. However, the ability to read a map is not only about survival; it helps you interpret what landmarks you're seeing and gives you a much clearer idea of what you're up for each day. If you are guide-free, it can also allow you to plot your own route, perhaps linking up different trails and paths, or even heading cross-country for short distances to avoid a road walk. There may be fascinating grottoes, cave art or waterfalls only a short detour off your path that you will blithely walk by if you aren't paying attention.

READING A MAP

All maps are magical, replete with the promise of adventure. Topographic maps—those that detail the three-dimensional shape of the land—are even more so, proffering not only adventure but control. Once you've deciphered its code (and worked out how to refold it), a topographical map gives you a wealth of information about the lie of the land that your path will cross. After a long walk, a topo map is a record of the walker's encounter with the landscape. The more detailed the better, so the ideal scale is 1:25,000 (where 1 cm represents 250 metres). However, a long-distance walk might cross over too many such maps, so 1:50,000

(1 cm = 500 metres) becomes more practicable, especially when you're following a waymarked path.

Every map shows a scale bar that makes it easier to gauge distances. With this and the edge of a sheet of paper, you can estimate the distance between the start and finish of your walk. Alternatively, by curving a piece of string (there's often one attached to a compass) you can accurately measure the length of your winding route. I love nothing more than fiddling about with string and I use this method to calculate distance for a proposed route or when writing up a walk for our guidebooks. On the path, when I need to quickly estimate how far remains to be walked, I use the grid that is usually printed on the map; counting the number of squares crossed by the path gives a rough reckoning of distance. Knowing my usual pace, I can gauge my progress or perhaps pick a likely spot for lunch. By using this technique and by keeping an eye on features of the landscape along the way, I have a fair idea of where I am on the map at any stage. Usually. If I'm paying attention.

As you walk, connect any new landmark—peak, village, bridge, stream—with a feature on the map. To do this, you need to be able to interpret the map's symbols and also its contour lines—the wavy lines that join points of equal height above sea level and so represent the relief of the terrain. An area where the lines are close together will be steep (bad luck); where they are far apart, the land slopes gently (hooray). Check the legend for the interval between contour lines (most likely 10, 20 or 50 metres) and count the lines from a marked value to see if you are looking at a hill or a valley. (Some kind mapmakers employ relief shading to help you visualise hills and valleys.) Once you get the hang of contour lines, you can pick out all sorts of landforms such as gullies and spurs, ridges, the saddle between two summits and, most importantly, cliffs.

Those grid lines mentioned earlier can also be used to refer to a position on the map by stating its *easting* (reading off the numbers along the bottom of the map) and then its *northing* (from the numbers along the map's sides). The ability to bandy about grid references in general conversation is invaluable— particularly if you're carrying a GPS device, as it talks to you in grid references.

Reading the map can become an obsession for some. Certainly, it's good to keep them close at hand when walking and a clear map case that hangs around your neck is ideal for this. Once, when walking on the South Downs—a swathe of green that drops into the English Channel in a most startling fashion—we were assailed by extremely strong winds. Our map, which had been snug in the outside pocket of my jacket, took flight and was last seen flapping its way to Boulogne-sur-Mer for an unscheduled holiday of its own. A map case would have prevented this but might have strangled me instead. Another option, and one that will have you looking less like a boy scout, is to refold the map so that the route is visible, protect it from rain by placing it in a plastic sleeve, then tuck it into the top of your pack or a *secure* pocket.

There's no point having the map accessible if you can't read it. John's glasses are always lost in one of the fourteen compartments of his pack so I am the navigator by default. That way, de fault is all mine if we go astray.

USING A COMPASS

The consensus of authorities on hiking is that you must learn how to use a compass. We always carry one and have a *theoretical* understanding of its uses . . . but to be honest we've seldom used it. In fact, it was only recently that we even discovered you need to have the appropriate compass for the part of the world in which you will be walking. On the several occasions when we pulled one out in Europe and found it strangely awry, we muttered something about iron ore in rocks affecting the magnetics and left it at that. Actually, our Australian compass was behaving predictably—we were just using it in the wrong world zone, of which there are five (it's something to do with the needle's vertical dip). As a result of not using a compass regularly, I'm employing this chapter to refresh my memory as much as yours.

The protractor compass—the type set in a baseplate—is light and easy to use. Most are made in Sweden where, presumably, people would otherwise stumble about in snowy white-outs and never get home to sup on their herrings. The essential thing is that a compass points to magnetic north (though this can be distorted by nearby metal objects), which lies on an island in the Canadian Arctic Archipelago. Unfortunately, the grid on your map doesn't point to magnetic north, but rather to the North Pole, and the difference varies according to your location. Anyone lucky enough to be walking in Wisconsin doesn't need to worry about this; there magnetic north and grid north are one and the same. Elsewhere, the magnetic variation is marked in a diagram on each map, and you should add or subtract this to your bearing. Ah! A bearing is simply the direction from one place to another, measured by the number of degrees it varies clockwise from north. There are 360 degrees in the compass rose (who would have expected poetic metaphor in this passage of certainties?), ranging from 0° (north) through 90° (east), 180° (south) and so on back to north again. Using numbers rather than cardinal points merely allows you to be more specific.

The function of the compass is to help you orient the map correctly and then read the ground more accurately. You may be able to orient the map by simply identifying landmarks around you. If not, lay the map flat and place your compass so that the side edge of the baseplate lies along a grid line running north. Then rotate the map and the compass until the north point of the needle (usually red) is east or west of the direction-of-travel arrow (the large one on the baseplate) by the number of degrees for that map's magnetic variation. It should now be easier to identify features in the surrounding landscape. An occasional quick glance at the compass can be used to confirm which section of the path you are most likely on; if you know you have been heading steadily west for some time and then veer decidedly north, you can identify a section of path that matches that manoeuvre. If the mapped path never heads west, you're in a spot of bother.

If you want to know your exact position on the path but don't have a GPS (and why should you?), here's what to do:

1 Select a landmark that you can see both on the ground and on the map and point the direction-of-travel arrow at it.
2 Twiddle the compass dial so that the N lines up with the red needle.

3   Add or subtract the relevant magnetic variation by turning the dial the relevant number of degrees. (I hear there's some good walking in Wisconsin, up near Lake Superior.)
4   Place the compass on the map with a side edge of the baseplate touching the mapped landmark.
5   Pivot the baseplate on the landmark until the arrow in the dial is parallel to the map's vertical grid lines.
6   Your position is where the edge of the baseplate intersects the line of the path.

If, by misfortune or misadventure, you have wandered off the path and wish keenly to know where you are, simply draw a line along the edge of the baseplate in the last step above and then repeat the whole process with a second landmark that lies in a different direction from the first. With any luck, you're where the two lines intersect. If you're planning to stay off the track and head into unfamiliar terrain, you'll need to use bearings and grid references and what-not to stay on course. Go and read up on it elsewhere.

READING THE PATH

How closely you need to read the path depends on its status. If it's an official long-distance path, your task will probably be very straightforward. If it's one of a network of walking paths in a forest or a national park, you may have to pay a little more attention. If it's a route cobbled together from rights-of-way, farm lanes and timber-getters' tracks, you may have to postpone the mental composition of the greatest novel of the twenty-first century and stay alert.

Official paths are usually signposted at major junctions, then waymarked with symbols that indicate changes in the direction of the path. The signpost might advise the distance to a hut or settlement and offer an estimated time to reach it. While these estimates are usually generous, you'll be able to adjust them for your own walking pace after you've encountered a few along the way. Some few are downright unreliable: I recall a series of signposts in the French Vosges that, in a clear display of *schadenfreude*, increased the time to the Col de la Schlucht the closer you got to it.

Waymarking conventions differ from country to country. The British use a no-nonsense yellow arrow for a footpath and a blue one for a bridleway (a path shared by walkers, bicycle riders and horse-riders). Norwegians opt for an enigmatic red T. The French are more expressive: long-distance GR paths (*grandes randonnées*) are marked with a red and a white stripe which can be bent to indicate a turn, or crossed to mark a wrong direction. Red and yellow stripes are used for a *sentier de pays*, a path that circuits the region. Single yellow, green or blue stripes waymark local walks. This system has been adopted in several adjoining countries, especially in mountainous areas. Switzerland stands firm with detailed yellow signposts that convey the impression that a bus will come along at any moment. Americans classically cut blazes into their trees for woodland trails but, in these days of greater sensitivity, are more likely to use metal discs or paint spots. Waymarks may appear on trees, boulders, fence posts, or anywhere that will catch the eye. Curiously, it is in villages and towns that waymarking is harder to follow, so you're most likely to get lost with a crowd watching.

The best waymarking is used with economy, appearing only when you might make an unfortunate decision. You may think that you could never have too many waymarks to guide you safely, but an excess can spoil the route and convey a patronising air. I have strong memories of an absurd abundance of marks across a landslip on the Europaweg, high above the Swiss Mattertal; there was so much red and white paint splashed on the rocks that the scene resembled a massacre of Arctic hares.

In treeless regions the waymarks may appear on posts or boulders, or there may be a series of cairns—small piles of rocks—to guide the way. Cairns are, to me, a thing of wonder. First, there's the word, which comes from the Gaelic *carn* and offers an excellent opportunity for 'r' rolling. Then there's the way a mere handful of small stones instantly makes a statement of human presence and, by implication, of human existence. Beyond that it has a cultural value: it suggests not the obvious 'I have made this' but, by social convention, 'you should go this way'. There's the sense of fellowship in the fact that some unknown person has made this for you and that you can trust that person. (By extension, the builder of misleading cairns is surely the most despicable of people.) Finally, there's the thing itself: an ordered pile in the middle of natural disorder, a simple rearrangement that makes you more aware of its context. Some Americans call small cairns for route-marking 'ducks'. There is no mystery in ducks.

A huge cairn at a mountain pass may also have another level of significance, apart from giving you something to aim for in bad weather. Early traders and others who crossed mountain ranges in trepidation often appeased mountain gods by adding a rock to a pile on the pass. The Incas did this to honour the *apus* or mountain deities in South America. The Japanese word for 'mountain pass' apparently has its origins in a verb meaning 'to offer', and what was offered was most often a small stone. Even for the godless, there's a sense of relief on reaching a high pass or a summit where a decent cairn sanctions the right to celebrate your achievement.

There are, of course, more prosaic matters to be dealt with. Sometimes a path will split in two for no immediately obvious reason. It may be that a tree has fallen across the original route or a landslip has occurred. If there's no sign to indicate otherwise, take the newer of the two routes, checking that it holds to the direction you would expect; it will probably be a good detour that rejoins the path beyond the obstacle. On a steep slope, however, avoid anything that looks like an unofficial shortcut, as using it will increase the chance of erosion.

In Australia, animal tracks can often mislead the walker: one minute you're striding along a narrow footpath and the next you're following a wombat through low scrub and into its burrow. In Africa, apparently, elephant trails can lead you astray in a similar manner (though, presumably, into a bigger burrow). Working woodlands can be crisscrossed by unmapped paths created by timber-cutters, hunters and, in Europe, mushroom collectors.

The times we take a wrong turn (and there have been more than one or two) are inevitably when we reach a junction and there are other people loitering there. In our haste to appear confident and in control, we wave a hello and rush on, failing to spot a vital waymark, or to consult our map. Risk mild embarrassment and pause at any such junction to make certain of your choices. Conversely, when you stop for a rest or food along the path, take care not to obscure a sign or waymark from others who pass by.

FOLLOWING WALK NOTES

When relying on written walk notes, bear in mind the fallibility of their creators, especially if the book is a first edition. My wonderfully innate sense of direction is matched only by my ability to confuse the words 'left' and 'right'—not a good thing in a writer of guidebooks. Surprisingly we haven't had too many angry letters; perhaps people are too lost to post them. If a direction doesn't make sense, check it against your map. The date of publication (of both map and book) is important, as features of a walk—especially man-made ones—can change over time.

The grading of a walk is entirely dependent on its context: a walk described in a leaflet aimed at passing tourists or family holidaymakers will be graded differently if included in a book for more enthusiastic walkers. In all publications, estimates of distance and height gain for a walk are just that. Someone has probably sat down with a piece of string to calculate distance. Height gain can be calculated these days with an altimeter, but the usually reliable author of a book I referred to recently had, for some sections, simply deducted the lowest point on the route from the highest, neglecting all the undulations in between.

At least distance and height can be measured accurately: walking time is a much more contentious matter. Mark Twain, after taking a steep walk up the Rigi-Kulm near Lucerne, wrote that:

> as Mr. Baedeker requests all tourists to call his attention to any errors which they may find in his guide-books, I dropped him a line to inform him that when he said the foot-journey from Wäggis to the summit was only three hours and a quarter, he missed it by just about three days.

Take any estimated walking times with a grain of salt. Check the front matter of the relevant book to see how walking times are calculated, and specifically whether or not rest breaks are included. Over a full day, breaks for food and rest can add up to some hours.

You'll get more out of walk notes if you're familiar with landscape terminology. Some guides include a glossary of foreign terms that are handy for interpreting maps abroad. No matter where you are, directions that make reference to 'true right' or 'true left' when discussing river banks assume you're looking downstream at the time.

One last thing to say about using walk notes: walking a route in reverse can be quite tricky. Sometimes a route is described in one direction for a good reason—prevailing winds, tricky descents, or so on—but often it's simply tradition, or one writer's whim, and it may suit your larger travel plans to walk it in reverse. If a linear route involves an overall height loss, review the timing for walking it in reverse. Pencil the route onto your map and rely more on that than on the notes. Walking backwards won't help.

ASKING DIRECTIONS

With the exception of Robert Louis Stevenson, this appears to be a male/female thing. John would rather die of starvation and have his decomposing flesh torn to shreds by the razor beaks of vultures than ask someone the way. He claims you have a fifty per cent chance of being given misinformation, not by intentional deceit but in confusion or error.

The chance of success can, however, be improved by asking specific questions rather than the vague 'where are we?' or 'where is my destination?' Questions that require a yes or no answer are ideal, particularly if you're not fluent in the local language. Pointing at the map a lot and raising your eyebrows can produce mixed results. If you have a few phrases, speak them slowly so the asked person is left in no doubt that you are either an idiot or a foreigner; that way he or she might respond slowly. If you fail to understand instructions given, at least you can start heading off in the direction pointed.

You risk very little by asking directions but can gain an awful lot. Once when we were slightly lost in olive groves on a hillside in Umbria we approached an old man harvesting wild asparagus and asked him the way to the village of Poreta. He pointed in the one direction that we thought it definitely wasn't, which was unfortunate. However, he also asked where we were from and when we replied he bellowed 'Owstraalia!' and nearly stifled us both in a bear hug. It transpired that Giuseppe had worked on the railways in South Australia for years, sending money home to put his children through university before returning to Umbria. His daughter is now an archaeologist and his son trained as a dentist. (Giuseppe deserved a better return on his investment: his smile was delightfully crazy, with toothy gaps and strange angles.)

The olive farmer insisted that we come and see his nearby home, which proved extremely modest. A telephone and hot running water were unknown luxuries, but a complete tour took some time: we were shown the room where three Polish youths sleep during the olive harvest, the olive-pressing room with vats containing the remnants of last year's oil, the pig pen, the device for slaughtering pigs, and the small room where bits of ex-pig hung to cure. Giuseppe was visibly fond of his three live pigs, each of which boasted a name, whereas his cat he called 'cat'. We weren't invited in to the main room of the house as his wife was resting (actually, he confided sheepishly, she was really his girlfriend; they were committing the sin of cohabitation, she at the tender age of eighty-four years, he at seventy-eight). The tour completed, Giuseppe brought out a high-domed loaf of his cheese bread, an Easter specialty, and said that we must just taste it. Immense slabs were cut, one for us to eat, washed down with homemade wine, and one to take on our journey. When it was time to move on, Giuseppe insisted that we cut through his olive groves and waved us off fondly. We even found Poreta.

12. Obstacles and aids

· · · · · ·

Along walk is a curious juxtaposition of trials and triumphs. In relative terms, they may be small trials—sacrificing the comforts of home or sensing the limits of your lungs on a steep incline—but they are trials that some people prefer to eschew. In doing so, those non-walkers also forgo the joys of the fought-for vista or the quiet encounter with wildlife and the heightened pleasures of a warm shower and a hot meal. Once again, these gains are small in the grand scheme of things, but are greatly enhanced by the contrast. As Shakespeare put it, 'Sweet are the uses of adversity.'

A little too much adversity, however, can be a tiresome thing. Unless you're fond of hair shirts and self-flagellation, or you subscribe to a religion that demands harsh penitence, you can make good use of a variety of leg-ups on a walk. Some are fairly obvious: where there's a torrent across your path, take the bridge. Some are ethically loaded: if you need to get over an electric fence then you're already on questionable ground. Some are just a matter of personal choice. If your knees have already done good service, take the chairlift and don't fret over it.

MAN-MADE BARRIERS

There are some landholders who would constrain the walker's freedom. Farmers have been known to hang 'beware of the bull' signs on paddocks holding nothing more threatening than a Shetland pony. The military establishment, who seem to own huge swathes of land in all the most attractive places, are always keen to keep you off it. Sometimes, it's not even theirs. Descending a difficult footpath through forest high in the Bernese Oberland, we encountered an officious sign blocking the way: 'Path closed—wait!' it told us in both German and English. Not a soul in sight. We waited, as instructed, but there was neither sound nor sign of human activity. It was getting quite cold and rather late. How long had this sign been there? Was it a cruel joke of the Swiss, who are not widely renowned for a lively sense of humour? I'm not sure how much time passed before we proceeded, but dinner was calling. Some way below, we passed a camouflaged man lying in foliage and muttering into a walkie-talkie and, some way on, the other path-closed sign. I hope we didn't undermine the nation's security, but really . . .

Long walks often cross private property, either on long-established rights of way (some lead right through the farmyard, between chicken coop and cowshed), or when asserting the 'freedom to roam' over moorland or fell, a principle that applies across much of the countryside in Scotland, Sweden and Norway. Occasionally (read 'when you lose the path') you may have to get beyond some barrier, such as a drystone wall. These low walls, built without mortar, are testament to a dying skill, so you really don't want to unbuild one. The secret of clambering over a drystone wall 'without damage to you or to it is to press down in every move you make', according to British writer Adam Nicolson. 'Gravity alone holds it together, and anything pulled or pushed in a different direction from gravity will come away,' he explains. I have had occasion to put this advice into practice—following one of John's cunning diversions that also included a fording of a bitterly cold river—and can report that it is correct.

Barbed-wire fences indicate a particularly mean spirit, both from want of natural materials and a clearly cruel intention. My first suggestion is to look for a stile (more on this shortly). In the absence of one, find an item of clothing you've never been particularly fond of and lay it over the wire to clamber over, or remove your pack, jack up the lowest wire, abandon your dignity and roll under. Many electric fences are not switched on, but there can be a real *frisson* in ascertaining this. Those fences that are turned on usually have a hoosier, whereby a loop of wire can be lifted off a post and replaced behind you. Electric wands that meet across a track can usually be pushed open at coloured rubber sleeves and should spring back into position once you release them.

In countries where footpaths are treated under law as a public highway, landholders have an obligation to maintain access. Consequently, walkers must often negotiate constructs designed to baffle livestock but permit humans. Sheep aren't great thinkers so these are rarely very difficult, but they can give you pause after a period of mindless striding out. As a wayfarer, you'll encounter an awful lot of gates. My favourite is the 'kissing gate', a small gate hung in a V-shaped enclosure that is impossible for anything not on two legs. It can, however, prove tricky if you are grossly overweight or carrying a large pack; the latter state is more easily remedied. The fastenings on regular gates are immensely varied and may require your full attention. If one is too complicated and the hinges will bear it (and the landowner isn't in view), climb over. This saves extra trouble, as gates should always be closed behind you.

Alongside a gate, or in place of it, you may encounter the stile, a delightfully simple means of passing through a hedge, fence or wall. The purest example is the 'testing stile', a gap between two upright stones only wide enough to permit a single human leg. Then there are all kinds of ingenious structures, including short stepladders and flights of stones that jut out from a wall. Stiles are perfectly charming until you've hoisted yourself over more than five of them in a short space of time.

Cattle grids are flat grids of parallel bars, common on farm lanes in Australia, Canada and Scotland, that can be difficult if you have very short feet. They're best taken at a brisk pace with no pauses to reconsider your situation.

Crossing a road is not normally considered a major issue, but when you've been crossing unpopulated terrain for several days, a busy road can come as a bit of a shock. When we crossed northern England from coast to coast, we had to traverse the three major arterial motorways that flow up the island. For the first two we were provided with elaborate footbridges and we paused midway to look down smugly on the humming cars and their occupants. We were a tad less smug at the third crossing when we were offered no such aid and had to dash across eight lanes of snarling traffic. In the safety of the pub that night we read in our guide that this was the section of the route that claimed most casualties. The only tip I can offer is to check for oncoming traffic in the direction appropriate to the country in which you are walking—then go like the clappers.

CROSSING STREAMS

I have an unreasoned trust in authority and tend to assume that a bridge over a river will carry me safely to the other bank. When two-thirds of the planks on a suspension bridge are missing, however, you realise that personal safety isn't always assured. John usually sends me over first, on the grounds that I'm lighter, and I go, on the grounds that I'm braver. Our scariest footbridge was a tatty thing in Corsica with a sign advising that it only be used in times of spate, which rather undermined my blind faith. Best to cross any footbridge singly—especially rope footbridges that develop an unnerving sinusoidal motion, moving side-to-side and up-and-down.

After a downpour or snowmelt, a gentle trickle can turn into a torrent and your route may require you to cross where there is no bridge. Take time to find the safest place, detouring upstream if necessary. Scout along the bank: if the river braids into channels, cross at the widest and shallowest spot—the narrower the channel, the faster the current. You shouldn't cross a stony stream barefoot as even a small cut on the foot can become problematic. In cold conditions, it's better to remove your socks and keep your boots on so your dry socks will warm you up after the crossing. Trekking poles are a great aid for judging the depth ahead and for improving balance. If there's a risk of being swept off your feet, unclasp your pack's hip and chest belts so you can slip it off if necessary. Take short steps, making sure each foot is firmly planted before lifting the other. If the flow is strong, cross with a companion, grasping each other's wrist, and crossing side-on to the current.

All this is starting to smack of too much Biggles. Undoubtedly, you should abandon a river crossing if it looks at all dodgy. We once tried to ford the River Dee in Scotland to reach our night's destination of Braemar, which sits prettily in a large bend of the river. We reached a shoal mid-river (where we foolishly disturbed a colony of nesting oystercatchers, a breed renowned for their protectiveness of hatchlings) only to encounter a peat-dark raging channel yet to be crossed. We opted to set the birds squawking again and walk an extra ten kilometres.

MOVING GROUND

Very occasionally, walking routes cross steep slopes subject to avalanche or mudslide. There may be signboards warning you of the danger; if not, the sudden absence of trees or the presence of avalanche barriers is a bit of a giveaway. Traverse these sections quickly and don't stop to picnic midway, despite the clear view on offer. There is not much you can do if caught up in an avalanche. Archy, the cockroach who laboriously typed many columns for the New York *Sun* with the help of Don Marquis, discovered this while climbing Everest:

> may sixteen at one thousand feet
> i met an avalanche coming down
> as i was going up
> we compromised and this morning
> i am starting all over again

Archy got off lightly, all things considered. My mother had a contretemps with a small avalanche while mountaineering in Scotland and was partially scalped by her ice axe. Walking is a more prudent choice of activity—we have managed to avoid avalanches entirely and have only been troubled by minor earthquakes in Italy. The greatest trouble these posed was after the quakes, when a television crew, desperate for footage, quizzed us as we sat eating pizza in the piazza of Bevagna, a quiet village in Umbria. How had we, as visitors, coped with the *terremoto*? Had we changed our travel plans? Were we concerned for our wellbeing? As we had slept blissfully through the tremors, there wasn't a great deal I could tell the interviewer—and even less so in Italian—but we exploited what might be our sole chance to appear on Italian television and were rewarded by a tour (with camera crew in tow) of ancient monuments otherwise closed for repair.

ARTIFICIAL AIDS

Sometimes, walkers benefit from aids laid down for more utilitarian purposes. The paths we've taken have led us through a surprising number of tunnels, carved out originally for a railway or during the construction of a dam. A head-torch is invaluable in such cases and for once you can wear it without feeling silly. Watch out for puddles.

Plenty of metal work was left behind by troops in the Dolomites during the First World War. To supply Italian and Austrian forces who were contesting the border high up among the spires, a lot of cabling, ladders and metal rings were attached to the rock, creating 'iron ways' or *vie ferrate*. These are now popular as a means of giving ordinary walkers some of the aerial thrills usually reserved for climbers and mountaineers, with a simple harness affording the walker a degree of safety. New routes have been also set up using such aids in France and Sweden. In North America, a fixed cableway helps walkers ascend the east face of Yosemite's Half Dome (that's the rounded face, not the jaw-droppingly sharp one).

Metal ladders are not uncommon on high-level walks, installed to help you up or down a rock wall. The Aiguilles Rouges massif, opposite Mont Blanc, features an entertaining series of short ones. The Walkers' Haute Route has a remarkably long one, very vertical and with an airy midway step across to a second ladder to gain the pass, known fittingly as the Pas de Chèvres or 'goats' step'. If you don't like ladders, there are alternative, earth-bound routes for both of the above. If you do have a penchant for ladders and fixed chains, head to the High Tatras in Eastern Europe or to the Northern Drakensberg in Southern Africa.

GETTING A LIFT

On the boring bits of a long walk, there's no law against catching a bus to an interesting bit. No one will know and you will undoubtedly survive any pangs of guilt. This also applies to any height-gaining (or losing) transport in mountainous country such as cable cars, funicular railways or chairlifts. The latter are awkward to board with a large backpack; try to get one of your companions to go first and watch closely. Most likely you will have to nurse the pack on your knees. If you do feel inclined to walk, the ground below a chairlift can be a rich source of mobile phones and local coins.

Other forms of transport may also prove useful to the walker. If you're planning to hop off a bus in the middle of nowhere so as to pick up a footpath, have the map handy to show the driver on boarding, then sit near the front and track the journey as best you can. Public transport isn't always available to deliver you to the track head. In villages where there's no taxi, you might ask at the local bar or shop if someone can drive you for a fee. It's a lot safer than hitching because someone else knows of your arrangement. If we're facing a long road walk at the end of a day, we'll be particularly sociable on the path and be ready to accept the offer of a lift on reaching the car park.

The advent of electronic devices is a mixed blessing for the community of walkers. In the case of a real emergency they are a great aid, guiding rescue services to your location. Sadly, too many novices who've taken a hike now call for assistance on their mobile phone or, worse, set off a personal location beacon (a PLB sends a one-way signal that doesn't allow authorities to quiz the signaller before dispatching a rescue service). Only summon help if you cannot rescue yourself because someone in your party is severely injured or if you are lost and bad weather prevents you from becoming unlost. Being tired is not sufficient reason for initiating an expensive and inconvenient search and possibly risking the lives of emergency workers.

If you are in real trouble but have neither of the above devices, the international rescue signal might be some use in catching the attention of distant walkers. To call for help, make six short signals per minute, wait a minute and then repeat until you get a response. A blast on a whistle is fine, although in regions where the noise could be mistaken for the calls of a highly regular marmot you could shout instead. If your pack and clothing are tastefully subdued in colour, dig something bright from your pack and secure it to the outside to assist searchers. A shiny emergency blanket can attract attention, if you've remembered to pack one. Should a helicopter come by and you do need help, raise your arms above you in the manner of an evangelist and stay well clear of any landing site. This Y shape also signals 'yes' to any questions from the pilot. 'No' or 'we're doing fine and there's no need to land' is signalled by forming a diagonal line with one arm raised and one lowered.

Most standard travel insurance will cover the cost of unforeseen medical emergencies on a long walk, as long as you aren't mountaineering with serious equipment or canyoning or running with the bulls in Pamplona. Check this before you head off, as rescue from remote areas can be a costly affair, especially in America. I have yet to ride in a helicopter so I'd like to be conscious when I do.

13. Weathering well

......

On foot, the wayfarer is at liberty, or perhaps under compulsion, to watch the weather. Indoors, we go about our business, unaware, unconcerned and unconnected. Outside, we face the uncertainties of a changeable system controlled by huge whorls of moisture-laden air. The atmospheric system had great import for our ancestors: its patterns dictated where and when humankind could migrate, determined where human settlements flourished, and influenced the physical changes that appeared between races. After centuries of paying it relatively little attention, we must once again acknowledge the weather as a powerful force shaping life on the planet. As the planet warms, some regions will presumably become too warm to walk comfortably and there will be more extremes in weather conditions.

The climate of a particular region—the average weather that we can expect—determines its 'walking season' and may help you choose when to walk where. However, the details of the daily weather can shift dramatically and it's those details that you'll have to cope with. It's no coincidence that the worst weather often strikes when you're walking through the toughest terrain. How well you cope and how much you can turn what most people consider a difficulty into a galvanising ingredient depends on preparation and outlook. G.M. Trevelyan, the keen walker and historian, claimed that 'Change in weather should be made as welcome as change in scenery.' Even the melancholy John Ruskin, in a rare upbeat moment, remarked: 'There is really no such thing as bad weather, only different kinds of good weather.' It'll probably be the blizzards and thunderstorms that you remember best once you're tucked up safe at home—as long, that is, as you make it home.

READING THE SKY

Not everyone wants to know what's coming. British author Jerome K. Jerome grizzled, 'Who wants to be foretold the weather? It is bad enough when it comes, without our having the misery of knowing about it beforehand.' It's true that having heard a forecast seldom prevents me from attempting the next stage of a long walk but if I have a choice of route it can lead me to take the lower one; up high, wet weather will be wilder and low cloud may obstruct any views. A forecast also suits my Eeyore-ish approach to life: I like to know the worst so that any bright spots are a bonus.

In some places, forecasting the weather is a simple matter: local lore advises that when you can see the top of Ben Nevis, it's going to rain. When you can't see the top, it's raining. In fact, extremely detailed forecasts are available for this notorious peak and for other mountain areas, advising conditions at different heights, and these are usually on display in walkers' huts and visitor centres. A few key weather terms in the local language will come in handy if there's something nasty coming.

In the absence of an accurate forecast, you can make use of a few natural indicators. Old folklore provides some useful guidelines: *Red sky at night, shepherd's delight; red sky at morning, shepherd's warning* holds good for walkers as well as shepherds. *When high clouds and low in different paths go, be sure that they show it will soon rain and blow* is less pithy, but helpfully alludes to the fact that windshear (different wind directions at different heights) often precedes a storm. In general, look windward for your personal forecast or, if there's no discernible wind and you're mid-latitude, to the west, whence weather usually approaches.

Clouds and cloud changes are wonderful harbingers of approaching weather and reading them is a useful skill, plus a good way of annoying your companions. There are two main variables: their shape and altitude. The main clouds to remember are *stratus* (stretched), *cumulus* (heaped), *cirrus* (wispy) and *nimbus* (which just means rain-bearing cloud). When these are seen at different heights, they indicate different weather conditions, although a nimbus is always a nimbus. Cumulus, for example, are fluffy, cotton-ball clouds that indicate fair weather—but if they start growing vertically and become towering cumulonimbus, things are less wonderful and a storm is brewing. If the top develops into a cirrus shaped like an anvil, a violent storm is imminent. If there's a green tinge to your cumulonimbus, it could be about to dump hail. By now, you're probably drenched anyway. More useful as a predictor are high cirrus clouds, stretched by wind in an otherwise blue sky, which often foretell a cold change due in the next twenty-four hours. Cloudscapes that look like fish scales (and are accordingly called 'mackerel sky') are mid- or high-level cirrocumulus clouds that can either break up or thicken; the latter heralds a cold front. Altostratus (*alto* denoting mid-level) usually carry moisture, and if they thicken and become lower nimbostratus, a long period of rain is likely.

My favourite bit-player in the cloud scene is *lenticularis*, the lens-shaped cloud often seen loitering over the lee of mountain peaks. This orographic cloud is formed when air cools as it's forced to rise over a large obstacle. It looks stable, but really it's being continually renewed and it tells you that it's windy as hell up there.

SUNLIGHT

While walking at night has its peculiar pleasures, you should be aware of the daylight hours at your disposal before you set off. Don't, as Irish novelist William Trevor did, let night 'come down too soon when walking in the Alps'. Start out early if you have a demanding day's walk ahead. If, like me, you are not someone for whom joy naturally cometh in the morning, this may mean setting off before your usual sense of bonhomie has been fully established. Avoid conversation until you can be civil.

That walkers are, in general, a cheerful lot may be due to the amount of vitamin D we absorb; certainly, it's been shown that a lack of sunlight often brings on depression. The danger for us is that we'll get a tad too much and be irreparably damaged by ultraviolet rays. An amazing number of Europeans walk without a hat or much other cover. While walkers in Australia or Africa are generally at greater risk of sun damage, they aren't the only ones: at high altitudes anywhere, increased ultraviolet rays can burn, despite the cooler temperature that may put walkers off guard.

Even on overcast days, apply sunscreen liberally but avoid the forehead: sunscreen mixed with sweat can sting the eyes. Find a brand of sunscreen that you like the feel of, as you'll need to reapply it after a few hours. Wear a brimmed hat and protect your lips with lip salve. If using trekking poles, also protect the back of your hands. Be wary of burning rays bouncing up from water or from bright ground surfaces such as sand, pale stone, and especially snow. The latter can seriously damage your eyes, so wear sunglasses unless the sky is very overcast. With care, the worst you'll suffer will be a case of sock-mark, whereby your feet remain lily-white while the rest of you browns gently.

TEMPERATURE

People have their own comfortable temperature range. Choose your destination and timing to suit your own preference. When reading the forecast temperatures, keep in mind that you will neither be lolling by a swimming pool nor sitting snugly by a roaring fire. If your body's internal temperature varies more than a few degrees from the norm, things go seriously awry.

On a hot day, plan for shorter distances and, ideally, for a long shady break at the height of the day. Drink plenty of water and take advantage of streams to soak a cotton hat and a bandanna for your neck. This technique reduces your need to sweat and so keeps you more hydrated. Heat stress and a failure of the body to cool itself by sweating—perhaps due to dehydration or high humidity—can lead to exhaustion and malaise. Seek shade, apply a soaked bandanna to the troubled walker's neck and give the person plenty of water to drink. If the symptoms are severe—including a rapid pulse, shallow breathing, confusion, headaches and affected vision—the walker may have a case of heat stroke, which can lead to death unless their body is cooled by covering them with wet cloths or encouraging them to immerse themselves in water. Simpler, really, just to take it easy in hot conditions.

In general, the higher the altitude, the lower the temperature will be. While you are moving, cold is rarely a problem; the heat your activity generates is sufficient to keep you warm as long as you have adequate clothing. Make sure you eat well and stay warm when you stop for a break. Beware of overdressing as it can cause you to sweat and feel clammy; I prefer to wear shorts even in cold weather. Look after your extremities with warm socks, gloves and most importantly, a woollen or thermal cap—you can lose up to a third of your body heat through your head.

With insufficient or wet clothing in cold conditions, perhaps exacerbated by a high windchill, walkers are prone to hypothermia. Sufferers will probably be too exhausted and confused to realise what's happening, so it's up to their companions to diagnose the problem. The warning signs are listlessness, stumbling, unreasonableness (that's half the population) and a failure to respond to repeated questions (I'll just get the thermometer). You should stop or seek immediate protection from wind and rain, remove the walker's wet clothing and insulate them, ideally in a sleeping bag, then give them a hot, sweet drink followed by hot food.

A surprising number of my acquaintances suffer from Reynaud's disorder of the circulatory system, whereby in cold conditions extremities such as the fingers turn first blue, then yellow-white and numb. John appears to have acquired a mild case later in life and he suffers most when cold combines with wind and water, as tends to happen in a blizzard. In such conditions, keep fingers warm and dry with liner gloves and waterproof outer gloves.

WIND

Most winds come and go, but certain landforms produce winds that recur. As air blows towards a mountain range and is forced upwards, the wind speeds up and can produce lots of rain and snow. When winds pass the crest and head downhill they pick up momentum and, while usually dry, can be even more violent. This down-slope wind can be warm (the alpine *föhn* or *chinook* of Colorado) or cold (the *mistral* of southern France) and can often last for several days. Winds that blow in off deserts are understandably hot; the one that blows from the Sahara across to southern Europe is variously known as the *sirocco* in Italy and the *leveche* in Spain. Experiencing a local wind can be unpleasant, but is part and parcel of discovering a terrain.

Strong winds have a reputation for making people edgy and it is possible that a rapid drop in air pressure affects our tissues and joints. A more likely irritant for walkers, though, is the fact that your nose runs constantly, your ears ache and the toggles on your jacket keep slapping your face. A day out in strong wind can be exhausting, particularly if you're heading into one. A more insidious danger is that the chill factor of a strong wind can lower the temperature dramatically and induce hypothermia. Walkers in Patagonia often experience days of being chilled and battered by the Roaring Forties wind blowing straight from the Antarctic.

There are other risks. Winds along coastal escarpments can be especially buffeting, so you should stay well back from cliffs. Gales can be even more frightening in wooded country. We have been on a hike in the Australian Ettrema wilderness where we watched trees fall around us, and at a rest spot had a full pack lifted off a rocky outcrop and dumped into the creek below. If strong winds are forecast, stay at a lower altitude and away from cliff edges. Small people should consider themselves warned.

MOISTURE

Very low-lying stratus (or mist) can make navigation more difficult, but isn't usually inherently perilous. The one time I've felt endangered by fog was while traversing a forest in Liguria during boar-hunting season. We could hear the poc! poc! of Italian guns, and even though the legal onus lies with the hunter not to shoot the tourist this would have been small comfort engraved on a headstone. Accordingly we dug from our packs the white napkins that we'd pinched in business class (after a serendipitous upgrade) and waved them as banners while singing loudly. This is the only occasion when I have been actively encouraged to sing in the wild.

If you're on a long walk, expect rain and pack waterproof gear near to hand. It can be a bit gloomy starting a walk in the rain, but there are compensations: the earth smells fresh, vegetation is lush and any waterfalls along the way will put on a show. A day's rain is bearable as long as you have adequate waterproofing for yourself and your pack, and possibly even enjoyable if your destination is a dry and warm inn. Light rain can be held off your face with a brimmed hat, but don't postpone donning waterproofs until you are wet; better to have to remove them than to get damp and chilly, as the combination of being wet and also cold can have nasty consequences. More prolonged, heavy rain is less of a lark and the only sensible thing is to stay out of it.

Flash floods are another possibility after heavy rain. They most often occur near mountainous areas, where the slopes catch the moisture in the winds and funnel them down narrow gullies. Canyons, particularly in arid regions, should be avoided if heavy rain is forecast upstream.

If cumulonimbus clouds build to a height where ice crystals form, you could be in for a thunderstorm. These can happen anywhere that rain falls, but are most common on summer afternoons among mountains—another good reason to start walking early. Thunderstorms are usually short-lived and can be invigorating, lowering the temperature dramatically and refreshing the landscape. They can, however, be a little too invigorating for the rare walker who gets too close to the centre of one. Lightning strikes create thunder, and the sound travels about a kilometre every three seconds (or one mile every five seconds)—so by counting the interval between the strike and the following rumble you can estimate how far lightning is from you. Thunderstorms typically travel a kilometre every 90 seconds or so, and you should seek shelter if thunder can be heard within 30 seconds of a lightning flash.

Finding shelter may not be as easy as it sounds. Here are some tips:

- Seek clumps of trees, ditches or low ground.
- Avoid high outcrops, sharp cliff edges and isolated trees (we all knew that one).
- Avoid making yourself the high point of a flat, exposed space (obviously).
- Avoid water: the current runs through it (that's interesting).
- Don't linger in the doorway of cabins or shelter in a shallow cave (bugger).
- If you are in a group out in the open, spread out so there's a good ten metres or so between you.
- If caught on open ground, crouch as low as possible with your feet together (tricky, must practise this).
- If you have something to insulate you from the ground, crouch on that.
- This is one of the few occasions when walking poles aren't so useful; set well aside anything that is made of metal, including poles, penknives or a pack with a metal frame.
- Cover your ears with your hands to reduce hearing damage.

Look, it's highly unlikely that you'll get zapped—and there's some comfort in knowing that, of those who do, 80 per cent survive. If someone with you is struck, it is safe to handle them: they won't retain an electric charge. You should give CPR (cardiopulmonary resuscitation) to a victim who isn't breathing and treat any electrical burns as you would other burns: by immersing the area in cold water, then covering with a clean, dry dressing. Be aware that the victim may suffer impaired eyesight and/or hearing and may need assistance to walk safely. But, golly, they'll have a tale to tell when they get home.

The risk of a lightning strike (or human stupidity) sparking a forest fire should be considered after a long, dry spell in hot areas. This is not restricted to the Australian bush or the woodlands of North America: southern European regions such as Sardinia, Corsica, Greece, Provence, Liguria, Spain and Portugal can also endure fierce forest fires. However, if it is hot enough for fires to thrive, it will probably be too hot to walk in comfort anyway.

Hail happens when ice forms around a dust particle in a storm front, gets swept up by an updraft and goes round in this cycle until the storm can't support it and it drops on innocent passers-by. It's most common in mid-latitudes, which is pretty much where I live. If you're caught in the open, protect your head; hail can get unpleasantly large and sharp.

Snow is likewise formed around dust particles, but it's decidedly nicer than hail and walking in light snow can be a charming experience. A fall in Switzerland's Pennine Alps once dropped perfect snowflakes on us—you could clearly see their six sides and it was tempting to just stop and compare shapes. More often,

I encounter the refrozen, blobby kind of snow, which is pleasant enough unless it's being driven into your face by a sharp wind. Brush it off every so often and you might stay dry; otherwise, snow collects between you and the top of your pack and starts to leak into the seams. As long as you can keep warm and stay dry, a short blizzard can be stimulating. G.M. Trevelyan thought so: 'The fight against fiercer wind and snowstorm is amongst the highest joys of walking, and produces in shortest time the state of ecstasy.' This is, however, a somewhat extreme route to achieving bliss and I'm sure there are less taxing paths.

RAINBOWS

Not something you have to worry about, but it's always good to end a chapter on a positive note. Rainbows are surely one of the delights of being out of doors in moist weather. As Wordsworth put it:

> My heart leaps up when I behold
> A rainbow in the sky:
> So was it when my life began;
> So is it now I am a man;
> So be it when I shall grow old,
> Or let me die!
>
> (FROM 'THE RAINBOW')

I know rainbows are caused by the refraction of sunlight through rain particles in the air and that the light splits into the colours of the spectrum, but the scientific explanation seems sadly lacking, considering how jaw-dropping the phenomenon can be. Look for rainbows against a shower opposite the sun, most commonly in the late afternoon and evening. If you're lucky you might see a double rainbow, with a paler, secondary rainbow (with reversed colours) arcing over the main one and a dark band of sky in between. This is known as 'Alexander's band', after the ancient Greek whose attention it first caught (not after the jazz band of the early twentieth century).

But wait, there's more! Rainbows aren't simply delightful ephemera. They can also be used to forecast the weather: a rainbow in the morning foretells showers, while one late in the day heralds fine weather. Amazing stuff.

14. Health hazards

......

Don't let this chapter title frighten you unduly: walking is by nature a healthy activity and by walking a long way you'll discover a level of fitness you thought you might never witness again. There are, however, a few minor risks that arise and it's wise to be aware of these (alert but not alarmed).

The most likely health problem you will experience is a bad cold or a chest infection, which can be difficult to throw off if you're at altitude. Apart from a mishap John suffered with a blood infection and faulty heart valve—which could have happened to anyone anywhere—the worst we've suffered in twenty years of wayfaring is a sprained ankle and a very nasty case of constipation, both endured (luckily on different occasions) by John. The latter misfortune is referred to obliquely in our personal lore as 'the Menaggio incident', which brings us nicely to the first topic.

HYGIENE

When life is pared down to the basics and your body's performance is a daily concern, bowel movements become a valid topic of conversation. Indeed, there are whole books written on the subject of sanitation in the wild. Make use of a toilet when you see one as there may not be another for some time.

In the absence of facilities, you must learn to be flexible: apparently squatting is good for the human frame. Unless you are prepared to improvise with soft leaves, carry a small supply of toilet paper or tissues. All used paper should be buried, along with your output, in a 'cat-hole', a small hole dug for the purpose using your heel, a stick or a trekking pole, which is filled in afterwards. (There's only one thing worse than the sight of toilet paper by the side of the path and that's suffering from diarrhoea after drinking contaminated water; any toilet work should be conducted well away from any watercourse and from the path.) Paper takes time to decompose, so ideally you should double-bag used toilet paper and carry it out. Some environmentally aware organisations now issue trekkers with 'poo tubes' so that they leave nothing at all behind.

Counter to John's Menaggio experience, American medico Sherwood Gorbach once quipped, 'Travel broadens the mind and loosens the bowels.' This mixed blessing is a greater risk when walking in South America, Africa and southern Asia, in regions that have uneven standards of food hygiene. If you have a choice, avoid food or drink that has a high risk of being contaminated. On an organised trek, with no choice over what you eat, make sure the cook understands the principles of safe food preparation and handling. Be scrupulous about your personal hygiene: avoid touching the food you eat, but if you must, ensure your hands are clean and dry. Even mild diarrhoea is an unpleasant inconvenience for the walker. (In South America, my friend Lani halted suddenly on the path and exclaimed 'Shit!' Her partner Mike asked if she'd left something behind, but no, it turned out she was stating a fact rather than an emotion. Lani now recommends carrying wet wipes.) Most cases of diarrhoea will resolve within a couple of days, but it's important not to dehydrate, so drink plenty of fluids. Adding salt and sugar in a ratio of 1:8 to a glass of clean water is effective if you don't have any sachets of rehydration powder.

Tampons and sanitary napkins should be buried or carried out. Some women find menstruating on a long walk an inconvenience and I must say that changing a tampon in the wild is a less than wonderful experience. You might consider avoiding periods altogether by continual use of the contraceptive pill. While on the topic, menstruating women are at slightly more risk of being attacked by bears—so consider the pill option if you're planning to walk the Appalachian Trail.

Another precaution to consider before you head off (although one applicable to both sexes) is to get your teeth checked; dental problems in remote countrysides are a nightmare. While you're at it, get your hair cut as well.

Maintaining a level of hygiene on the path is sometimes difficult but always important. If running water is in short supply for washing hands, consider packing a tube of evaporating hand-sanitiser. If you get the chance to wash in a stream or lake, take it. Robert Louis Stevenson, after 'making his toilette' in the River

Tarn, enthused that 'To wash in one of God's rivers in the open air seems to me a sort of cheerful solemnity or semi-pagan act of worship.' Whether baptising yourself or your dirty clothes out of doors, be sparing with soap or detergent, particularly in slow-running water. Nowadays, you can carry eco-friendly cleansers. If full immersion is not possible due to severe cold or a strong current, use a corner of your mini-towel as a washer. At the least, washing the face, neck and armpits will do wonders for your morale.

In some huts, showers are available at a cost, often using a token rather than a coin. Two tips: first, discover how to operate the shower before you strip naked, and second, apply soap as soon as possible in case the water flow is brief. As a rule, wash yourself at the end of the day before you cool down. I have read that you should avoid soaking your feet in the morning, as the softened skin will be more prone to chafing and blistering. Another tip is to avoid using deodorant, as it is good for the system to sweat while exercising (and without the stresses of urban living you will be less whiffy anyway). Distance walking is not for those addicted to cosmetics; these are heavy to carry and the scent can, in American woodlands, attract the attention of—you guessed it—bears.

I tend to wash socks, knickers and my shirt overnight, making full use of hand basins in hotels or refuges. We carry a universal plug in case someone has decided to complicate life by removing the original, but a rolled-up sock can be a good substitute. Use whatever is to hand as detergent—soap or shampoo—or carry a tube of laundry concentrate for longer walks. If the weather is fine, a small towel and socks will dry quickly tied to the outside of your pack. The lower, muddy sections of zip-off trousers dry quickly and I figure the rest of the garment can wait until a return to civilisation; just don't inspect them too closely.

Incidentally, when you do get home, you should launder your jacket if it is made from a fabric such as Gore-Tex and you've sweated in it. Body oils can clog up the pores of the fabric; washing, followed by warm tumble drying and warm steam ironing renews the water repellence. Note to self: wash jacket.

FOOT AND LEG ISSUES

A walking excursion demands a great deal of your feet and legs. On occasion, they will fail to perform as well as you'd hoped. I am blessed with healthy feet; they are my best feature. I took them terribly for granted until I had occasion to compare feet with fellow walkers. My, there are some ugly examples out there. I'll try not to be smug and just offer some guidelines to make the most of what you have. Guideline one: cut your toenails. Guideline two: keep cutting them at regular intervals.

Blisters

Mercifully, we have managed to avoid blisters by wearing well-fitting boots and by treating symptoms early. Blisters are essentially small burns caused by friction, and the first sign of a coming blister is a red hot-spot. If this isn't covered with a sticking plaster or moleskin dressing (available from pharmacies), the hot-spot fills with fluid and blisters, at which stage a padded dressing around the blister may be helpful. If the blister ruptures, apply an antibiotic ointment, cover with a sterile dressing and check occasionally for signs of secondary infection.

During the First World War thousands of troops suffered from the disabling condition of trench foot. Wearing cold, damp socks in tight footwear for days on end can cause a painful restriction of blood flow and eventual damage. Even short periods of walking with wet feet can lead to blistering, so dry your feet carefully after washing or river crossings.

Leather boots suffer each time they have to dry and can crack and leak unless maintained along the way. Brush off any mud and dry the boots away from direct sun and heat. If you are not too cold, the best method is to don dry socks and let the warmth of your foot dry your boots from inside. I carry a repair kit of an old toothbrush head and a small amount of leather conditioner; check what is suitable for your boots.

Where possible, make it a habit to remove your boots and socks at lunch time to give your feet some quality time.

Muscles and ligaments

To be honest, I don't bother stretching. It seems to me that, unless you have to ascend steeply from your doorstep, the act of walking is sufficient warm-up for the act of walking. Others believe it is worthwhile stretching the calf muscles by pushing against a wall or a boulder with one bent leg in front of the other, pulling the back calf taut, and then swapping legs. I promise not to laugh or call you Sisyphus.

I once developed a nasty case of swollen tendons, having tied my boots too tightly around bloated ankles the day after a long-haul flight. After a couple of days spent padding the back of the ankles, I resorted to walking in my reef sandals. This wasn't too bad in sunny Brittany, but I don't recommend a 35 km walk in them. My tendons remained tender for the next few weeks and I've been very careful about boot lacing ever since, adjusting the laces after the first half hour or so. Just before walking down a long hill, tighten your laces a little so that your ankles are better supported.

Unrelated but not easily covered elsewhere is the condition of Walker's Hands. Actually I just made up this name to denote that unpleasant, heavy feeling you can get when you're not using walking poles and the blood pools in your hands down by your sides. I'm not fabulating this, it happens to other people too in hot weather. Relieve the discomfort by tucking your thumbs in your pack's shoulder straps at chest height for a while.

Sprains, fractures and other nasties

Injuries are most likely to beset you when you're tired and not attending to where you're stepping. Take breaks to rest, eat and drink so that you reduce the risk of a fall. Sprained ankles usually occur going downhill, but don't be cavalier on what looks easy ground: John twisted his ankle after stepping into a divot on otherwise flat pasture and coming down awkwardly under the weight of his pack. To minimise the swelling of a sprain, soak the joint in cold water (or apply a bandanna soaked in water) then elevate it on a pack. Keep the boot on if you have to walk out; otherwise, wrap tape or a bandage around the foot and wind it up the ankle. We now carry an ankle and a knee support; such items can be beneficial on a long descent.

It's unlikely you'll have to deal with anything worse, but it's good to be emotionally prepared and not faint away at the first sign of trouble (or blood). If a fellow walker has suffered a serious fall, do not move them if there's any chance of spinal injury. If they are conscious and have a fractured bone, you should immobilise it by improvising a splint (from trekking poles, a tree branch, a rolled-up sleeping mat or other) and binding it to the limb with bandages or cloths. Any open wound should be covered, with pressure applied to stop bleeding; a bandanna serves well as a large bandage.

A short first aid course would be a good investment before heading off on an independent walk.

TOO MUCH WEATHER

Less dramatic but more likely is that you'll suffer minor ill effects of excess weather exposure: sunburn or a mild case of heat stress or chill. An irritating consequence of cold and windy conditions is that your nose can run like an open tap. Keep blowing it on paper tissues and you'll have pocketfuls of soggy waste to weigh you down. Keep blowing it on anything at all and you'll get a raw nose susceptible, if you're like me, to cold sores. So, if you're in the great outdoors and away from other human beings, you have licence to air-blow your runny nose. I apologise if this concept offends. Just make sure you don't blow into the wind.

If you're heading to the very high hills, you may have to deal with the consequences of oxygen deprivation: air at altitude carries considerably less oxygen than at sea level. Unless you were born and bred in the mountains, your body will start to work less effectively once you are above 2500 metres. At such altitude you might experience headaches and fatigue, although most people won't suffer any noticeable effects until considerably higher. Several days acclimatising before undertaking strenuous activity will help. Drink plenty of water and limit your intake of alcohol, the effects of which increase with height. Sleeping at a lower level than you reach during the day tends to reduce ill effects.

As this book is not for mountaineers, I won't trouble you with symptoms of acute mountain sickness and cerebral oedema (vomiting, hallucinations, nonsensical babbling, stupor, coma, death). (Is death a symptom?) Some popular walks in South America (the Inca Trail and the Cordillera Blanca), Africa (Mount Kenya, Mount Meru and Kilimanjaro), and many in the Himalaya do take non-mountaineers up to great heights. If you're undertaking such a walk at altitude you should be wary of pulmonary oedema: the accumulation of fluid in the lungs, which has symptoms akin to pneumonia. If you start coughing up pinkish foam, you could be drowning in your own bodily fluids. For all of these types of altitude sickness there is only one cure: get the hell downhill. However, you might want to carry preventive drugs that can be prescribed by your doctor.

GETTING BITTEN
This is one of our big primal fears, so let's start with small things and work upwards.

Insects
Annoying insects thrive in the strangest places: mosquitoes can be a problem in Iceland, gnats in Mongolia and midges in the Scottish Highlands. By New Zealand's Dart River there's a hut

named for the persistent locals—Sandfly Hut—with a cunning double door to keep them out.

I have a net veil for wearing over a hat if I'm walking where such irritations exist; it looks ridiculous but I'm the only one laughing when we stop to eat lunch and others get a mouthful of additional protein.

I wouldn't normally single out brand names but one body product with a surprising side effect is worth a mention. The general store in the Scottish village of Crianlarich sold us an Avon moisturiser named 'Skin So Soft' to ward off midges, and strangely enough it did the trick for the remainder of the West Highland Way. It turned out that the product's midge-repelling power was common local knowledge, and its sweet odour on the trail would often herald the approach of even the burliest hikers.

In tropical regions, especially in low-lying pasture, mosquitoes carry the threat of malaria and other unpleasant diseases. Chemical prevention is complicated and regionally specific so consult a doctor specialising in travel medicine or a tour organiser before walking in the tropics.

I live in an area rich in tick life and get bitten frequently; friends refer to me as a tick-magnet. Normally this isn't a big concern: you simply grasp the tick close to the skin with tweezers, then twist and pull. (Once, though, I must have stood on a nest and had to remove over a hundred larval ticks. For two weeks my ankles resembled those of someone suffering from elephantiasis.) Mature paralysis ticks release a toxin that can give you a nasty headache. John botched the removal of one such tick from my head and I got the full dose: within minutes I turned bright red and developed large welts on my arms and upper legs. An antihistamine soothed the reaction and I haven't suffered anything like it since, despite several bites. Apparently, the transmission of any disease such as Lyme disease or Rocky Mountain spotted fever usually occurs near the end of feeding, so there's a good reason for getting ticks off early. Ticks often crawl around on you for some time before selecting the tenderest or most embarrassing spot to bite, so to reduce the risk of being bitten, cover up when walking through a likely habitat and then check yourself and clothing afterwards.

In hot and humid climates, leeches can be an unwanted distraction. They aren't dangerous, but they do employ an anticoagulant that may cause the wound to bleed for a while after you've pulled off the leech (or once the blood-swollen blob has dropped off). Take care that the site doesn't get infected, and avoid scratching it. Some walkers wash their socks in salt water to discourage leeches, some cover up with gaiters; I just keep an eye on my boots when in leech territory.

Spiders and snakes

Spiders that spin webs are rarely very venomous (I'm sure I read that somewhere), so you're unlikely to walk into danger that way. Deadly spiders are more often found in dark corners, so be careful where you put your hands when rock scrambling, collecting firewood or using an outdoor toilet.

In some countries, you might encounter snakes, sunning themselves on a rock or on the track; we see potentially lethal ones frequently on walks close to home. Few snakes are aggressive:

some may get antsy if they feel threatened, but their bite may not inject much venom. Few bite above the ankles, so high boots or long trousers offer some protection. In warmer months, keep an eye on the path and you'll be fine.

Having said this, any bite should be taken seriously, and the victim should be reassured and kept still. If they were bitten by an elapid snake (that includes cobras, mambas and all venomous Australian snakes), the affected limb should be bandaged snugly, starting from the fingers or toes and working all the way up to the torso, putting a mark on the bandage to indicate the site of the bite; handy compression bandages are available that indicate the ideal pressure. If you're walking elsewhere and the bite was from the viper family (that includes adders, rattlesnakes and coral snakes), just immobilise the limb. Someone else should go for help; bad luck to those walking solo.

In Europe, the only venomous snake is the adder and its bite is only lethal if you suffer an allergic shock reaction. Australia, people like to think, is a veritable pit of death-inducing snakes and spiders; we also have killer jellyfish, octopuses and stingrays, but these are unlikely to trouble the walker unless they are severely off-track. Surprisingly few travellers die from snake bites, but if you have an irrational phobia, consider walking on islands certified free of venomous snakes, such as Iceland, Ireland, Crete, New Zealand and Madagascar.

Large biting wildlife

Among the brochures of commercial trekking companies I perused, one advertised an African safari on foot. This is surely asking for trouble. While walkers have few natural predators, you are advised not to actively seek them out.

Those who choose to walk in North America may have to contend with bears. These come in two types: the black bear and the grizzly. The former can be warded off by talking loudly and waving your arms above your head; the latter should in no manner be aroused. A friend who was planning to hike in Alaska read up on this ahead of departure. He returned—surprisingly, in the circumstances—to tell us that from a distance it is extremely difficult for the bear-novice to tell the species apart and hence to take any action at all apart from losing bladder control. He also told us a joke in which a park ranger warns potential hikers to sew bells on their cap so as not to alarm a bear into defensive action. When asked if there are many bears in the park, the ranger assures them that the number of scats indicates there are. When asked further how the hikers can identify a bear scat, the ranger replies, 'They're the ones with little bells in them.' At least I hope it's a joke.

There's no outrunning a bear. Should one attack, you might manage to beat off a black bear (ah! a new use for trekking poles) but not a grizzly. If a grizzly decides to charge at you, you're supposed to stand still in the hope that it is bluffing. If it isn't and it lays a paw on you, you should play dead. Luckily, fainting will achieve the same effect. Food, toothpaste and other strongly scented things (does this include socks?) should be hung up from the bough of a tree or stored in a bear-proof container, well away from your tent. You are advised to eat in a third location, presumably allowing the bear to rummage through your tent without interruption after getting riled by your smelly socks dangling from a tree.

Lacking the threat of bears or lethal snakes, the British walker has found something else to obsess over: dogs. Any guidebook penned by a Brit is sure to refer to dogs as the walker's bane. Robert Louis Stevenson started it off: 'I respect dogs much in the domestic circle; but on the highway, or sleeping afield, I both detest and fear them.' The British hiker is particularly afeared of continental dogs, which can presumably sniff a Channel-crosser at great range. It's true that dogs can be a nuisance. Crossing pasture high above the Amalfi Coast, we were rounded up by three dogs guarding some goats. Their teamwork was impressive: one barked a constant threat, the second leapt about in front of us while the third appeared from nowhere and nipped my calf. And then they vanished, leaving me with a crescent bruise but no puncture mark. The fact that they targeted me and left John unscathed confirms my theory: they could scent British blood. Luckily, such working dogs are rarely infected with rabies and, as long as you have had a tetanus shot, an altercation is unlikely to be fatal. For the nervous, there are personal devices known as 'dog dazers' that scare canines off with high-pitched screeching. Others might consider throwing stones or defending themselves with a trekking pole.

Apart from the Amalfi encounter, all our doggy issues have been the converse: a case of extreme friendliness and desire to go for a walk. A shaggy black thing followed us halfway across Corsica before, to our relief, adopting another couple heading back in the other direction. Europe once had its share of more dangerous animals, including voracious wolves. A giant wolf known as the Beast of Gévaudan terrorised the Aubrac region of France during the 1760s, consuming large quantities of women and children who might have survived had dog dazers been available back then.

A final word on something that won't bite, but may induce a heart attack: the grouse. This incredibly annoying bird lies low in heather until you are within a few metres of it and then explodes into the air in a cacophony of sound and feathers. If you survive this, you'll survive anything a walk can throw at you.

15. *Walking etiquette*
......

One of the most striking aspects of a long walk is the natural camaraderie that arises along the path. There is also the strange but welcome phenomenon of social levelling in operation. Once, while admiring Toulouse-Lautrec's artworks in Albi in southern France, we overheard two Americans greeting each other for the first time: they promptly established name and state of origin, then occupation and exact level of remuneration, all within several minutes. The conversation was ridiculous in the setting of a gallery, but it would have been obscene on a walking track.

On the path, all people are recreated equal, unless they are wearing unsuitable shoes. Not equally loveable, mind you. I do recall repeatedly encountering a less than appealing family of four on a route across Corsica. The father had a voice that could strip paint and the two grown sons were bearish dimwits. All four filled the dormitory on successive nights with a stridor of snoring. We encountered them one last time at a confusing junction and made our choice of path simply so as to lose them. Sometimes evasive action is the only sensible option.

A long walk usually brings out the best in us all, but some people, stressed unduly by physical challenges, allow their sense of self-preservation to take over. My friend Sue has just returned from an organised trek in Nepal, which was tarnished by open hostilities within the party, leading almost to blows. There's absolutely no point bickering with other walkers if you can't avoid them. Your dealings with others can make a walk more or less enjoyable for everyone and, in some cases, can be a matter of safety. If individual styles of walking differ markedly, consider the words of G.M. Trevelyan: 'There is no orthodoxy in walking. It is a land of many paths and no-paths, where everyone goes his own and is right.'

Walkers are casual visitors to rural and remote regions and, in their dealings with those who live there, should behave with the grace of a good guest. In poorer countries, it's important not to flaunt your wealth to people who may have no concept of walking as a leisure activity. You'll find that old-fashioned conventions of courtesy still have currency in any out-of-the-way place. And courtesy shouldn't be underrated. Hilaire Belloc went as far as to versify:

> Of Courtesy, it is much less
> Than Courage of Heart or Holiness,

Yet in my Walks it seems to me
That the Grace of God is in Courtesy.
(FROM 'COURTESY')

BEING DISCREET

As a general rule, you should give other people plenty of space—
after all, that's why you're all out there. Unless there's limited sitting
room, there's no need to crowd together at lunch like vultures.
Likewise, give others a turn to enjoy a peak or viewpoint in
peace. The last time I climbed the highest mountain on Australia's
mainland (Kosciuszko, which at 2228 metres, admittedly isn't very
high) it was to find dozens of teenagers waving flags and singing
the national anthem really badly (it was Australia Day).

Being quiet on the path gives you a better chance of seeing
wildlife. Moreover, it's embarrassing to be caught talking too loudly
about something as mundane as farting habits by a stranger who
pops out from a switchback. (Farting, by the way, is permissible
as long as it is performed silently and downwind.) Sharing half a
mobile phone conversation is bad enough on a bus; it's even more
ridiculous in the wild. Keep any phone switched off while it's in
your pack and only use it when other walkers aren't around.

There is also the matter of visual indiscretion. Travellers are
often advised to dress so as not to offend in foreign countries, but
there should be more specific warnings for walkers. Older hikers
should be cautioned against micro shorts, and *lederhosen* should
be banned outright. T-shirts bearing nationalistic logos involving
hearts are also prohibited. John has a Foreign Legion–style cap
that is highly dubious, but that's more a matter of poor taste

than deliberate offence. Traditionalists regard anything that isn't murky green or dirt-brown as an affront, whereas I think a bit of colour adds a nice touch. Certainly fluoro pink and lurid lime are a little startling on the path.

Night brings other etiquette issues. In another part of our Snowy Mountains, a fellow hiker pitched his tent smack-bang next to ours while reminding us that his snoring sounds like a koala in heat. We moved. If you know you snore, please don't drink copious quantities of red wine before falling into your bunk or sleeping bag. Sharing a cramped hut requires a certain level of consideration from everyone to make it bearable, never more so than when the weather turns bad and there is a tussle for space to hang dripping garments while the sour smell of damp socks pervades the room. At such times, dig deep into your reserves of civility and be determinedly pleasant.

MEETING WALKERS

Along the path, no matter which country you walk in, you'll meet Dutch folk—tall and thin with glasses—presumably walking where you are because their own country is so flat. Dutch walkers are very pleasant and usually know more about everything than you do but don't make a big deal of it. Actually, all walkers are a notch above their fellow countryfolk, and as a walkers' hut can be a mixing pot of nations (albeit well-off nations), it's a good way to meet people in general.

If you've picked your route well, whole days can go by without the sight of other walkers on the path, but there are inevitably busier sections, especially where day-walks are feasible. The custom among walkers is to convey a greeting as you pass: a smile and a nod or a few words suffice. In fact a few words is too many, as the walkers' greeting is necessarily brief: *hola* in Spanish, *salve* in Italian and in German *Grüss Gott*, which looks long but is reduced to something more like *'sgot'*. My friend Karen thinks you should say *hi* or even *g'day* to indicate nationality, but I prefer to pretend I've mastered the local language. If someone on the path fails to respond, you'll know they've just arrived from a city and hopped out of their car for a view and don't have the pure soul of a 'proper' walker.

By custom, if walkers meet on a narrow path, those coming downhill should make way for those ascending. On the level, a meeting can be something of a Chip-and-Dale affair: 'After you' . . . 'No I insist, after you.' It makes sense for larger parties to defer to smaller ones. On the occasions when you want to overtake a slow walker or a large group, catch their attention with a greeting or a cough: it's quite unnerving to be pushed past by someone unexpectedly on a narrow path. Wait your turn patiently, however, when crossing a footbridge, an avalanche zone, or any other area where walkers need to concentrate or where safety is an issue.

Keep sufficient space between you and other walkers so you don't tread on their feet or lose an eye if a branch flicks back. Pole manners are very important: those using trekking poles should mind where the tips are pointing, particularly when tucking them under an arm. When a scramble up or down a steep slope is necessary, walkers should wait until the slope is clear. If you dislodge rocks that might strike any walkers below, yell 'Rock!' as loudly as you can; this might give someone time to at least protect their head if not move out of the way. There is no need to follow the churlish example of British mountaineer Edward Whymper, who, on being the first to reach the summit of the Matterhorn, actively hurled rocks onto the competing Italian party below.

I'm not one for long social encounters when afoot. We have several times walked in Europe with Paul and Gigi, who will chat at great length to everyone they meet at a junction—it is admittedly how we met them in the first instance—but I can rarely give such conversations serious attention as my feet are usually itching to get on. On the other hand, there is great pleasure in company at the end of the day, something Robert Louis Stevenson sums up nicely: 'it seems as if a hot walk has purged you, more than of anything else, of all narrowness and pride, and left curiosity to play its part freely, as in a child or a man of science'. The ideal company for the evening is that of fellow walkers, with whom stories can be exchanged, routes compared and useful tips shared.

ENCOUNTERING LOCALS

Also important to your adventure is the local population, upon whom you will be relying for supplies and perhaps lodging. Back in 1711, Joseph Addison remarked on the difference between the manners of city-dwellers and those of countryfolk, the latter retaining the good behaviour of an earlier age: 'A polite country squire shall make you as many bows in half an hour, as would serve a courtier for a week.' Although bowing has died out, be prepared for more polite formalities in rural areas and among other cultures. Walking in another era, Robert Louis Stevenson treated the Cévennes peasants as a different species. Not only were they from a different social class but they spoke a strange dialect of French. He was, on occasion, downright rude and drew an appropriate response.

At least Stevenson could speak French. In an ideal world, you would always be fluent in the local language, but the tongue's failure to flow shouldn't deter you from walking in a particular region. My school French and evening-class Italian have each coagulated sadly over the years. In 1875 *A Manual of Etiquette* advised: 'Converse with a foreigner in his own language. If not competent to do so, apologize, and beg permission to speak in English.' This only works, of course, as long as the other party is versed in English. You will undoubtedly survive without any shared language but you are more likely to thrive if you can deliver a trickle of useful words and phrases. You might even enjoy yourself more.

On most organised treks, you will benefit from the close company of locals. Check that any guides and porters are paid good wages (and, ideally, life insurance) and that they have adequate clothing and footwear. Some companies pay low wages and levy a separate 'gratuity' that should be budgeted for. Companies running regular walks through disadvantaged countries often give something back to the local communities by supporting education or charitable causes. Give your business to one with a good record, even if they charge a little extra. Interestingly, people with the least are often the most friendly. We found a grizzled herder in the Abruzzo hills particularly chatty, though admittedly he'd had only the conversation of goats for some time.

Some locals, however, are best avoided. If you hear gunfire during hunting season, whistle loudly and wave something white as you walk. If it's not hunting season, a running pace might be more appropriate. (We once spent an eerie hour following a trail of fresh bloodspots that ended abruptly in a splatter, with no sign of victim or victor.) Natives can be troublesome in other ways. Mark Twain, walking in the Swiss Alps, was thrilled to hear a young shepherd boy delivering the 'famous Alpine *jodel* in its own native wilds' and he gave the lad a franc to continue awhile. 'After that', he writes:

> we found a jodler every ten minutes; we gave the first one eight cents, the second one six cents, the third one four, the fourth one a penny, contributed nothing to Nos. 5, 6 and 7, and during the remainder of the day hired the rest of the jodlers, at a franc apiece, not to jodel any more.

In some countries, denizens go a step further than yodelling and throw dangers of theft, banditry or political conflict into the path of the walker. Find another path.

Hamlets and villages should pose no problems and may well offer succour. In my experience, locals are far more appreciative of walkers who have made the effort to reach them on foot than they are of bus-deposited tourists or other motorised travellers. In small settlements, a polite greeting to passers-by is welcome and may even stimulate a conversation. Walking into a larger town after several days of limited human contact is a surreal experience and gives you some empathy for space aliens. It's best to take things slowly: find a bakery and order a little something rather than dashing into a supermarket where you will be disoriented by the remarkable range of toothpastes and their gaudy packaging. Don't bother trying to fit in when passing through a large town: any attempt will fail and you will simply look like the village idiot in need of a bath. Instead, wear your boots with pride and ignore the fact that everyone else in the café is endowed with poise and style and doesn't have hat-hair. Sadly, any smiles or greetings offered to passers-by here will most likely be met with a raised eyebrow.

CONSIDERING THE LAND

Many of the best paths skirt or cross private land on rights-of-way. When walking these, make a point of sticking to the route as closely as possible, closing gates carefully and disturbing farm animals as little as possible. Never, for example, get between a sheep and its lamb, no matter how much you'd like to take the lamb with you. And never get between a cow and a bull, for obvious reasons. According to experienced rambler H.D. Westacott, 'the bull is a clumsy animal and, providing you keep calm, it should be possible to dodge if it does charge'. If a landowner challenges you, it's best not to argue but rather to retreat with apologies. As guidebook author Alfred Wainwright advised, 'In his own field, a bull is always right. On his own land, a farmer is always right.'

Earlier in this book I mentioned a few techniques for making a low impact underfoot. The premise that walkers should leave no trace extends to the environment alongside the path. Take a plastic bag for the purpose of carrying out all rubbish; if you can manage it, this extends to picking up the detritus of others. Pay strict attention to fire bans and, at other times, avoid lighting fires unless you have absolute control over them (Henry David Thoreau once started a forest fire, to his great shame). Leave flowers where they grow; draw a picture of them instead. Walk in small groups, choosing trekking companies that limit the size; apart from it being a more pleasant experience, you'll have less impact on the natural surroundings.

If all visitors to national parks treated the environment with the same respect there would be fewer regulations imposed on walkers. And although it's likely no one will reproach you for small environmental misdemeanours, remember that, added up, such minor acts will inevitably spoil the beauty that has brought you all this way.

16. *Along the way*
......

Once the techniques of walking and of navigating have been mastered, the matters of food and shelter are taken care of, and you're confident enough to relax, you might find yourself casting about for something to occupy your thoughts. Looking at the scenery is well and good but, at a walking pace, it changes very slowly and can seem much the same as yesterday's. Informing yourself about what you're looking at is the best way of making a scene more accessible, or 'readable'. First though, let's consider some more frivolous possibilities.

CONVERSATION
According to Mark Twain, 'The true charm of pedestrianism does not lie in the walking, or in the scenery, but in the talking.' Twain's bold statement opens up a big debate. If the scenery is

stunning, surely you don't want to be distracted by chatter. If the conversation is deeply engaging, having to watch your footholds or losing your breath on a steep climb can only interfere with a careful thread of words. What I enjoy when walking is neither small talk nor existential debate, but something in between.

In the opinion of Max Beerbohm, writing in 1918, sensible conversation is quite out of the question. He argues that walking for walking's sake (whereby your legs are 'merely bandying you about to gratify the pride of the soul') does not stimulate thought but rather stops the brain altogether. As evidence, he describes a pattern in which a man who has 'the power to instruct or amuse when he is sitting on a chair, or standing on a hearth-rug' loses it as soon as he takes someone out for a walk. All the conversation that same man can muster is a few pleasantries and then he is reduced to reading aloud any inscription that they pass, including milestones ('Uxminster 11 miles') and public notices ('Drive slowly'). Aha, you say, the problem for Max must be the pool from which he draws his company. No—one of his close friends was Oscar Wilde, who could have turned even a 'Trespassers will be prosecuted' sign into a razor-sharp *bon mot*. Presumably Oscar wasn't the walking type.

Sharing the third corner of the ring are William Hazlitt and our friend Robert Louis Stevenson. Both are for walking alone, mainly for the very reason that conversation isn't an option. 'I cannot see the wit of walking and talking at the same time. When I am in the country, I wish to vegetate like the country,' says Hazlitt. By all accounts, he was a blunt man. Stevenson was more enlightening on the desired vegetative state, explaining that it does not involve logical thought (or internal conversation) but quite the opposite:

> And so long as a man is reasoning he cannot surrender himself to that fine intoxication that comes of much motion in the open air, that begins in a sort of dazzle and sluggishness of the brain, and ends in a peace that surpasses comprehension.

Whatever your own thoughts on this matter, a narrow path requires walkers to proceed single file, making conversation less straightforward, especially if the range of your hearing is diminishing as rapidly as mine (a tip: walk in front). As a result, there will be plenty of times when not conversing is a sensible option and this is, in fact, a good thing, as long as you enjoy your own company. If you're not overly taken with yourself, you will need some other distraction.

ENTERTAINING YOURSELF

On those occasions when you are in want of light entertainment, you might consider singing. Hazlitt, despite his reputation as a churl, occasionally did:

> Give me a clear blue sky over my head, and the green turf beneath my feet, a winding road before me, and a three hours' march to dinner—and then to thinking! It is hard if I cannot start some game on these lone heaths. I laugh, I run, I leap, I sing for joy.

A great advantage of the outdoors is that there's less chance of annoying others while exercising your voice, although you should ensure that any wind is blowing away from nearby settlements. To keep you cracking along there are plenty of good rhythmic songs to choose from: songs to thresh the corn by or to march by, sea shanties for when everyone had to row together, and waulking songs. (That's not a misprint; these were songs for women weaving at their looms.) If you're more modern in your tastes, you can rummage through the popular hits of your youth. If you can't remember the lyrics, make them up.

Should you find that your new lyrics have merit, you could go that next step and compose poetry. After all, someone has to do it or the world will be an impoverished place. There are plenty of walking precedents: all the Romantic poets were walkers, even Lord Byron, who had the excuse of a misshapen foot and two deformed Achilles tendons. As Freud complained, 'Everywhere I go I find a poet has been there before me.' You don't even have to master rhyme: Walt Whitman didn't bother. And in sharp contradiction to Max Beerbohm, Friedrich Nietzsche stated that 'All truly great thoughts are conceived by walking.' So, go to it.

The privation I most deeply feel on a walking excursion is the loss of music. For an extended period, I must get by without the haunting melodies of Patty Griffin, the wise riffs of Richard Thompson and the sublime voice of Youssou n'Dour. You might suggest I load all these musicians onto a small device and have them walk along with me. It's not impossible; I am, it is true, happily falling behind the times, but I'm not a complete technophobe. Yet there is something unfitting in seeking closer contact with the natural world while your ear is plugged into a lump of electronica. Apart from the antisocial nature of such behaviour, Youssou, Richard and Patty would distract me from being where I am. Besides, they give me some motivation to eventually return home.

In the place of music, there's much to be said for listening to the surrounding sounds: water trickling, trees rustling, birds calling, animals piping an alarm, wild boars rutting . . . Apparently, trees do not simply rustle. In *Under the Greenwood Tree* Thomas Hardy wrote that every species of tree can be distinguished by its 'voice':

> At the passing of the breeze, the fir-trees sob and moan no less distinctly than they rock; the holly whistles as it battles with itself; the ash hisses amid its quiverings; the beech rustles while its flat boughs rise and fall.

When something less natural disturbs this new-found peace, you'll probably find yourself most indignant. National air forces always pick the most beautiful spots to exercise their sound-splitting planes; at least there will be one upside of future fuel shortages.

Inevitably, at some point on a long walk, the human need to enforce order on chaos will prevail and someone will start proposing lists. It might be a list of something obvious—the top ten albums released in 1969 or your favourite ten novels featuring a chicken—but you could veer the discussion to something more fitting for the occasion: your top ten lake walks, top ten non-mountain rambles or perhaps your top ten lunch spots on walks. However you will need to complete at least ten walks before you can fully enjoy this pastime. At the back of the book you'll find several of my top-ten-walks lists as they currently stand; I look forward to revising these constantly over the coming years.

EDIFICATION

The less curiosity you have, the less rewarding a walk will be; it's a simple equation, but an undeniable one. If you can't find interest in what you walk past, a long-distance hike will seem very long indeed. If you take the trouble to assemble and digest a few relevant facts between trips, that body of knowledge will enhance your walking experiences and give you new insights into your environment. Edifying yourself becomes more than a means of virtuous self-improvement: it has the potential to stave off boredom and engender enthusiasm.

Admittedly, factual information is a dry business until you can use it to interpret what you are actually seeing. 'A danger of travel,' philosopher Alain de Botton complains, 'is that we see things at the wrong time, before we have had the chance to build up the necessary receptivity and when new information is therefore as useless and fugitive as necklace beads without a connecting chain.' De Botton, however, has foremost in mind an excursion through a city crammed with varied architecture and historic monuments from different periods. The wayfarer on foot has a much easier task, spending days to cover a relatively short distance that contains far fewer elements. It becomes possible to perceive the shared features of barns built in one valley and then to discern these from those in the next, separated by a high pass. This ability may not be of much practical use back in the office, but who knows when you'll be walking through another barn-rich district?

A significant but simple step in learning about your surroundings is learning the names of the local features. Don't wait until you're lost to get out the map: name the settlements, peaks and valleys that you can see from your rest spot. True, place names are mere labels, but labels help us to create a mental map and they usually have some significance. It helps if you can translate them: I blithely walked below Schreckhorn in the Bernese Alps without knowing that its name meant 'peak of terror' (or that my father had climbed it sixty years earlier). Knowing names can only give you greater insight into a landscape.

Geology

Geology isn't just rocks, it's the whole shebang: Earth's origin and story, its materials, processes and dynamics. Admittedly, this large subject is best broken down and handled in smaller chunks, starting with the ground beneath your feet. First, there are igneous rocks—records of thermal activity—cooked under the earth's surface and thrown up in volcanic eruptions or revealed by erosion. Erosion, caused by the action of water, produces fragments that are then moved about by rivers and seas and deposited in layers as sedimentary rocks. Changes in pressure and temperature, often due to the movement of tectonic plates, transform igneous and sedimentary rocks into—you guessed it—metamorphic rocks. So if you can identify the rocks you skip over (or come to grips with if you're scrambling up a steep slope), you might guess at what once transpired in the vicinity: whether a volcano spat, whether a sea ebbed, whether ancient continents collided. I think that's wonderful. Even when you can't see the rock for soil, the plants that grow will give you clues, as different soil types create a habitat that suits particular plants.

This is a field of interest for which every walk provides more material, as minerals and natural forces behave predictably wherever they interact. Most clearly visible is the shaping power of water, but you needn't be on a weathered mountain pass or in a river-cut canyon to see signs of that. Sinkholes indicate a karst landscape, where soluble rock has been eroded by water moving under the ground. Strange grooves in a smooth rock face suggest the grinding passage of an ancient glacier. Elsewhere, large boulders or 'erratics' lie far from their point of geological origin, plucked from the bedrock by a passing glacier and later abandoned like lonely giants. Well inland, we often discover sandstone overhangs that are embedded with shell fragments. The other day I walked down a near-dry stream bed, pocked with potholes that had been eroded by sand and pebbles whirled around by eddying water over millennia. Small-scale scenes like this can be as humbling as a towering mountain range.

Botany

Wildflowers and their appreciation are one of the great pleasures of walking and it's a field of study in which a little effort is well rewarded. Small yellow flowers that were all much of a muchness when you started walking can shortly be differentiated and even identified. This process can be sped up dramatically by glancing at flora charts on the refuge wall at night, or by thumbing through those reference books on the bookshelf. Even better is a quick visit to a local botanic garden where plants are clearly labelled. As an alternative to buying a heavy field guide, you might pick up a leaflet from a national park office. Most flowers can be tracked down by their colour, save for a few species which cunningly change hue during the flowering period. Leaf shape can prove useful for identification when a flower's shape and colour are too common. In alpine areas, you'll find that most flowers—regardless of their colour—are some species of gentian, with the exception of saxifrage, which isn't.

Don't trouble too much over scientific names or your companions will find you tedious, but you'll find that common names can be wonderfully entertaining. One delicate flower I photographed on the last adventure bears the appellation of 'great masterwort'. Meanwhile, a bizarre primitive plant that the French playfully call *joubarbe à toile d'araignee* (beard of Jupiter with cobwebs) is known to the English simply as house leek. Australian names can sometimes be misleading—the coastal flower known as pig face deserves better—but we were more inventive with a red-flowering vine known as running postman. In tropical climes, the flora gets really showy.

Trees, though sometimes less eye-catching than flowers, feature in almost all landscapes, having adapted to a huge range of environments. Conifers can withstand harsh conditions with a snow-shedding shape, evergreen leaves and pollination by wind. Deciduous trees grow in less hostile habitats, often bearing fragrant flowers to encourage pollination by insects and growing broader leaves to intercept more light. In dry regions, silvery leaves reduce water loss; in wet areas, tapered tips allow water to drop quickly. Palms aren't strictly trees but they're interesting nonetheless.

Once you've ascertained whether a tree is a conifer or a broadleaf (bad luck, palms), identification is a matter of leaf shape, where terms like 'lobed', 'toothed' and 'pinnate' come into play. If you can't see the leaves, you can closely inspect the bark of the trunk. Regardless of whether that helps, it's a nice thing to do.

Fungi are a much overlooked kingdom. They can be very colourful and deserve further consideration—particularly before consumption.

Fauna

There are few thrills greater than watching an animal in its natural environment. Some people take holidays with this express purpose, maximising their chances of seeing wildlife; for walkers it is an added benefit of being in the right place at the right time. It's fascinating to witness how animals have evolved to fill the evolutionary niches offered by a particular landscape. The further you walk, the more you'll see. A coastal walk offers the chance of seeing dolphins, seals and, greatest of all, whales. Woodlands may house squirrels, deer, pine martens or foxes. Above the treeline, other animals appear: hares, bovids (I had to look that one up), marmots. This last, a relative of the squirrel, is a charmer: on sunny mountain slopes across the northern hemisphere you'll often hear the warning whistle before you spot a fat marmot hurrying to safety.

It's good to know beforehand what other animals inhabit a region so that you're more alert to signs of them. Wild animals often use footpaths to traverse country, so you'll likely see tracks and scats in snow, sand or muddy stretches. Field guides usually include a chart of tracks to distinguish one species from another; if you don't have one, photograph the tracks and refer to a book later. The best place to look for animals is by water, either still or flowing. Animals are more conspicuous in national parks or reserves where they are protected; in such places they will allow you to approach much closer. In the Aiguilles Rouges natural reserve, we encountered a marmot that, I swear, must be in the pay of the reserve's authority. While not straying far from the entrance to his burrow, he went through an entire routine—standing alert on tiptoes, having a quick wash, munching a pawful of grass, scratching himself—while we stood a few metres away. It wouldn't have surprised us if he'd passed the hat around.

The ideal time for animal spying is either early morning (counts me out) or late afternoon (thank goodness). In Australia, many larger animals are nocturnal, so night-spotting—wandering around pointing a strong torch into the trees—can be rewarding. Some animals are notoriously shy no matter what the time. I've only seen the tracks of a lynx, the pointy stumps gnawed by a beaver, and the carcasses of a recently deceased badger and platypus, none of which are quite the same as seeing the live version. Animal sightings have also often been a great compensation for us in indifferent weather. We once counted 98 alpine salamanders on a ridge walk in the Bernese Alps; low cloud prevented us from seeing anything much else, living or otherwise, but those salamanders were some consolation. Low cloud also provides a better chance of getting nearer to larger animals and has given us all our close encounters with shy chamois. A warning: time can pass very quickly when you're gazing at a moose or an otter, so be aware of how long you have left to reach your destination. If you are lucky enough to see animals in the wild, you'll no doubt be spurred to read more about their habits: where they sleep, how they rear their young, and so on.

Bird-watchers have a reputation as obsessive people disconnected from the real world and this is, on the whole, a fair assessment. It certainly describes those of my friends who can tell a spotted rock warbler from a red-necked dotterel. However, a healthy interest in local birdlife (one where you don't feel compelled to tick all the boxes in a bird book) is only natural, and quite likely to develop in walkers. It's a very portable interest as there are birds to be seen pretty much everywhere, except in Italy where they have all been shot. Birds are seldom willing to assist in your study: they usually keep their distance and refuse to stay put. Patience, however, will be rewarded, and your ability to observe size, beak shape and leg colour and to distinguish calls can only improve. A pair of compact binoculars will help. If you want to identify a particular bird, confer with a companion on the details to confirm a mental image, or take a reference photo. Later, you can look it up in a field guide: just don't start ticking boxes. The best place to start is with raptors, since they are large and hard to miss: condors, eagles, vultures and smaller birds of prey are all very striking, so to speak. Work your way down in size and, eventually, you may even identify some of those little brown things.

Walking through different habitats—atop seacliffs, over moors, lakeside—increases your chances of seeing a range of birdlife. A scramble up Ben Nevis, Britain's highest mountain, via the Carn Mór Dearg arête, was made even more special by the appearance of a pair of snow buntings, found only above the treeline. In new territory where you're unfamiliar with the rarity or otherwise of a species, each bird earns its due: we got very excited to spot a bird of exotic markings in woodland, located the glamorous French name and then, only later, learned it was a jay. I don't know whether they're common or not (there's an awful lot of colour on the distribution map) but it didn't reduce the pleasure of watching it.

We are spoilt for birdlife in Australia, with numerous showy parrots and a huge chorus of songbirds. For bushwalkers, the ultimate passerine pleasure is the sound of a male lyrebird in action. This large bird performs for the girls by throwing his lyre-shaped tail over his head and mimicking the calls of many other birds in a continuous song that may also include other bits and pieces he has overheard. Walking on is quite impossible until the show has ended.

Local history

There aren't many places on Earth that humankind hasn't ventured into and, if not settled, at least made use of a few resources (there are disused mines in the most surprising places). It often suits us to ignore remnant evidence of such activities, preferring to pretend that we're walking in wilderness, but we can take a different stance and find interest in signs of human endeavour and in what they tell us of life in a sometimes harsh environment.

For me, the most fascinating relics are those that have no obvious utility: stone circles, rock art, huge figures cut into chalk hills, Easter Island's statues. They don't have to be prehistoric. We've occasionally happened upon elaborate towers of carefully sorted and stacked stones that would have taken hours to erect. On Ireland's Burren, we found dozens of tiny dolmens mimicking the real ones nearby. These edifices aren't waymarks, nor are they a personal tag like a name carved into rock or tree; and while I know you should leave a landscape untouched, these expressions of an interaction with the natural world appear rather special. Some people would call them signs of human spirituality or religiosity; I prefer to think of them as acts of imagination.

Acts of imagination often follow a tradition and, combined, become expressions of culture. The opportunity to read up about traditions of another place or time will give you a better understanding of sites that you pass through, be they the ruins of a Premonstratensian abbey or contemporary Buddhist shrines adorned with fluttering prayer flags. Interestingly, the other major marker of landscapes is human conflict. Contention over borders produces fortifications in remarkable settings. When we've stumbled on these unprepared, it was hard to comprehend why blood was spilt. When we've arrived better informed, it has sometimes made even less sense. The history of human conflict, be it religious persecution, ethnic disagreement or simple land-grabbing, adds a thought-provoking element to a walk and puts life in some perspective.

Stargazing
True, this isn't a subject to pursue while actually walking, although many writers—including Dickens, Trevelyan and Coleridge—

heartily recommend a night stroll. Unfortunately, star visibility is best on moonless, cloud-free nights, making the walking part tricky. Walt Whitman mused in his poem 'Night on the Prairies', 'I walk by myself—I stand and look at the stars, which I think now I never realized before.' There was a good reason for this—Whitman living, as he did, in Brooklyn. The wayfarer usually has the advantage of being in a location well away from the urban glow of light pollution.

If you're going to be serious, don't try standing and craning your neck; lie down on a sleeping bag or lean back on your pack and have a good gaze. With the naked eye, thousands of stars should be visible. If you have binoculars, you should see even more. A star chart will help you to identify constellations, which never bear the slightest resemblance to the thing for which they're named. The brightest planets are Venus, Mars and Jupiter. The planets used to be something you could rely on, but since they've demoted Pluto, I've lost a bit of confidence in the solar system. I do know that while stars twinkle, planets merely reflect sunlight. Those walking in the southern hemisphere have a good view of the three brightest stars—Sirius, Canopus and Alpha Centauri—and of the Milky Way. Luckily, everyone is well placed to see the moon.

Satellites appear like a steadily moving star, but can be confused with a plane. Keep an eye open for 'shooting stars': meteors that burn up as they enter the atmosphere. Large ones leave a bright bolide or trail, the colour of which can differ depending on the rock's mineral composition. Meteors occur more often than you would expect—luckily most of them don't hit the ground and get upgraded to meteorites. A shower of meteors is a particular treat and recurring ones can be planned for; you might want to be in the countryside when the Leonids put on a show around mid November each year.

Cloudspotting

One thing not to take up too seriously while walking is cloud-spotting, as this will only lead to tragedy. By all means, keep an eye on what clouds are about and whether or not you should be preparing for a blizzard, but leave the 'Look! there's a cart-wheeling llama' type of cloudspotting for when you're lying down after the day's walk and you have no further need for your sense of balance.

Not everyone sees the point of industriously seeking greater knowledge of nature by naming and categorising it, à la the Victorian movement. John Fowles, in an essay contemplating trees, argues that 'this dreadfully serious and puritanical approach' deters us by making nature the subject of a school lesson. Even worse, Fowles believes, 'the far saner eighteenth-century attitude, which viewed nature as a mirror for philosophers, as an evoker of emotion, as a pleasure, a poem, was forgotten' and that Darwin made 'sentimental innocence, nature as mainly personal or aesthetic experience, vaguely wicked'. Can't we have it both ways? Is it possible to walk with one eye appraising the beauty of the scene while the other scans for order and causality, without developing a level of schizophrenia? Or do we have to switch between modes of observation? Happily, Fowles discovered that there was less conflict than I had imagined between nature as external assembly of names and facts and nature as internal feeling; that the two modes of seeing or knowing could in fact marry and take place almost simultaneously, and enrich each other.

Leave some space for an emotional reaction to what you're seeing, be it the minutiae or the larger picture.

Perhaps we should take a tip from the young. Among the manifold contents of nephew Jez's pack was a kite. On an evening stroll around a high Swiss lake, it bobbed and wove frivolously and made us all forget our tired limbs and look skyward for a change.

17. Recording the walk
......

There are several reasons why anyone would wish to record the details of a long walk. The obvious one is that, assuming you've enjoyed the overall experience, you'll want to revisit it in detail and, in so doing, perhaps regain something of the pleasure you felt at the time. You might want to entertain friends and family by sharing sights and tales so that the viewer or listener gets a sense of what it was like to be there. A more selfish reason, but one perfectly understandable, is that you'll want to impress them with your hiking prowess. For you to do any of the above well, you'll need to record a few details first. This chapter is concerned with doing that in an interesting and effective way.

The simplest means of recording a walk is to annotate the map. This may be just a matter of plotting your route onto it, if it is not already featured, or of showing any deviations that you made, intentional or otherwise. You might indicate day stages and their duration, overnight stops, highlights, where you saw ospreys, and so on. You would first have to overcome that common reluctance to despoil the printed page, but if this is to be your only record of the trip, despoil away. If there's insufficient space on the map for what you want to add, draw a personal sketch map that recreates your walk. Ooh, there's a bold word: 'recreates'.

We tend to think that the ability to recompose the world around us—whether in words or as an image—is a gift that some people (usually others) have received. That's nonsense. Australian writer Helen Garner, when interviewed, said, 'To me the difference between the artist and the non-artist is that the artist is the one that does it.' Just as we can learn new ways of seeing and interpreting, we can also develop techniques of recreating and preserving. When you have good material to work with—a pleasing landscape, a day full of activity and small incident—what's needed to do it justice is not some wafty, intangible creativity but a degree of palpable skill.

DRAWING THE JOURNEY

Perhaps the best illustration of this is the very act of drawing. We all used to be able to draw when we were children and then we stopped, frozen by self-awareness. It may take some longer than others to rediscover this ability, but perseverance is usually rewarded. The nineteenth-century activist John Ruskin dedicated much effort to teaching working-class adults the basics of drawing: shading, perspective, framing and so on. He believed that drawing could teach people to appreciate detail or, as Alain de Botton would have it, 'to notice rather than to look'. For Ruskin, drawing was a means of understanding and so possessing the beauty of a landscape or a village. While this might seem ambitious, no one is hurt in the attempt.

The doyen of walker-sketchers was Alfred Wainwright, whose many books on rambling in the north of England are filled with perfect copperplate text, hand-drawn maps that magically become sketches at the skyline, and detailed pen-and-ink drawings of landforms and rustic buildings. He does a lovely cairn. There is little body text as such, only blocks of observation with captions revealing wry humour: 'lane fit for cricket' annotates a map; a side-on diagram of a bull is for the benefit of 'junior hikers'. Sadly, we can't all be Wainwrights, but I still take pleasure in sketching the odd scene.

Only limited equipment is required for this activity. For pencil drawing, you'll need a light pencil (such as a 2B) for sketching outlines and a soft, dark pencil (perhaps a 4B) for shading and toning. You'll also want a small sharpener (or a penknife) and an eraser that can be used as a 'reverse pencil' to create highlights. A pad of drawing paper should be small; pages that are too large will get battered in the pack. Cut a rectangle in a small piece of black card and you have a handy viewfinder for composing a landscape. If you have confidence in your hand, take a single pencil for sketching a layout, but then work with technical ink pens—ideal for recording fine detail and creating crisp lines. You only need two black ink pens (a fine nib and a broader one) plus a thumb for smudging shadows. Alternatively, take a few coloured pens which, as long as they're not toxic, can be turned into watercolours with a bit of spit on the page. Just make sure you store any ink pens in a plastic bag or your entire wardrobe could become an artistic statement.

During the day's walk, you'll have to be content with quick sketches rather than elaborate drawings if you want to reach the destination in time for dinner. With more leisure in the evening, you might draw the scene outside your hut. Plot a layout and draw rough outlines, then hatch in shape and forms before developing details, especially in the foreground, with small, irregular lines. The landscape will often provide a fine subject, but at times your focus could fall on a plant or a farmhouse or on fellow walkers. Look for strong shapes and interesting textures or patterns. With limited time, make use of white space—the blank areas of the paper—to imply shapes with simple lines and so create an impact. Don't overwork it; it's important to know when to stop drawing.

PHOTOGRAPHY ON FOOT

Ruskin was of the opinion that a camera could not do justice to a scene, and it wasn't simply because the daguerreotypes and glass plates of his day were technically inadequate. He believed that the act of taking a photograph prevented people from looking at something properly. Today, when a camera lens clicks in an instant and we can take hundreds of photos at little expense, his argument is even stronger. Hasty snapshots can inhibit us from looking closely, but I believe that careful photography encourages it. Attempting to convey the atmosphere of a place and the essence of what it makes you feel is a serious goal. The acts of selecting the subject, composing the picture and harnessing the lighting are choices that can elevate your pictures from simple records to personal recreations.

Good photography takes time, which is something a lot of travellers don't allow themselves. On foot, however, you can wait for the light to change, or you can walk just a little way up the path to improve the angle.

Camera kit

Digital cameras are a boon for walkers. I took a long time to give up my much-loved film camera but, as a technically challenged photographer, I soon appreciated the immediate feedback that a digital camera gives me and the facility to freely take extra shots for correction or experimentation. After a few years, I even sat down to read the manual and am now starting to use my camera as it was intended.

The gap between compact cameras and single-lens reflex cameras (SLRs) is narrowing; a good compact allows you to exercise control over exposure, colour balance and focus. For many walkers, an SLR is too bulky and heavy but if you can fit it in, an SLR gives you a precise viewfinder and the ability to swap lenses. I carry two lenses: an 18–55 mm and a 90–300 mm (admittedly there is a bit of a gap between them, and an even wider lens would be nice). Become familiar with your camera before you start walking, ideally at a time when you can experiment with various challenges. Failing that, a long plane flight can be a good time to review the myriad settings.

You will need to carry spare batteries or to locate power sources to recharge a battery pack along the way, possibly a problem in more remote regions. Some cameras allow you to turn off the preview option, which will save a lot of battery power. If your batteries do fail on the path, you can often nurse them along simply by wiping the contact points. Batteries often misbehave in very cold conditions, so keeping the whole camera tucked in your jacket on such occasions helps. They also don't cope well with very hot, humid conditions.

Digital storage cards are wonderfully lightweight after carrying rolls of film for years. I used to limit myself to 30 slides a day; now I just make a rough but generous calculation and buy any extra cards before departing. I keep my camera set at the highest possible resolution and delete any absolute duds each evening.

To best capture detailed shots, especially in low light, you need some means of keeping the camera still. A full-sized tripod is impractical, but a mini-tripod with flexible arms can be easily positioned on your pack or a rock. Some trekking poles have a mount for a camera on the handle, and using such a monopod prevents vertical movement. A cable or wireless release will avoid any jarring of the shutter button.

Two filters—an ultraviolet filter for haze and a polarising filter for water and rich colours—can improve landscape photographs and also protect an expensive lens from scratches. Attach the lens cap to the body of your camera with tape and string so that you don't leave it on a rock; over the years I've picked up numerous lens caps along the path. A cleaning cloth or fine brush completes your kit.

Whatever camera you carry, it's of no use to you buried deep within your pack. Our friend Brett walks with his camera in his hand, but then he is looking for an excuse to upgrade. I carry mine around my waist in a padded camera bag with a top that opens right up. It has a divider to protect the spare lens and a flat pocket for small bits and pieces. It rests against my belly and allows me to change lenses easily and cleanly. The only downside of this arrangement is that the pressure of it bouncing on my bladder as I walk reduces my ability to hold out for a piss.

Camera gear has to be protected from the elements. In light rain or snow I whip a lightweight shower cap over the bag. If the rain persists, I stop and bury the whole camera bag in my backpack and swap it for John's compact camera, which I keep tucked inside the neck of my rain jacket. At the time, it may seem a chore to take pictures in awful conditions, but later you'll regret not having that record of friends on the top of the pass, or an evocative shot of those granite fingers that you followed through the mist. To protect your camera from moisture, you could use the plastic bag method: cut a small hole in the bottom of a clear plastic bag and poke the lens through this, securing it with a rubber band, and operate the camera through the original opening. It's not only rain that can cause problems: salt water is especially harmful, so on coastal walks, protect your camera from sea spray. Keep it well away from sand, as well as any grit and dust blowing about.

Content and composition

Choosing your subject and positioning it within the frame are matters of judgement that improve over time. There are various guidelines—don't put the focal point in the very centre of the frame; fill the viewfinder with the subject; don't let extraneous things creep in at the edges; keep the horizon straight; think about foreground, middle ground and background—but these are not hard-and-fast rules. Personal taste plays a large part in composition. I have a penchant for shooting vertically, partly because I may need to include a picture in a portrait-format book, but also because I think that particular orientation challenges the viewer more. Horizontal (or landscape) format will, on the other hand, display better on your computer. I also like making the sky a feature of a composition, lowering the horizon in the frame. Interesting or ominous clouds can make a dramatic subject. Over a long walk, you'll see a lot of sky and horizon.

Sweeping landscapes can be exhilarating to experience, but lose a lot through the camera. Every photograph needs a point of interest to draw the eye. Often a landscape is improved by including people to give a sense of scale. In such cases, they should ideally stand in the middle distance and be looking at the scenery rather than at you; this also helps to convey the act of moving through a landscape. Take this a step further and deliberately take shots where the theme itself is 'walking'. I didn't take enough of these early on and I regret it. The path itself can also be an interesting subject, and sometimes including a walker obscures too much of it (or distracts from it if they've got a lurid backpack). I often take a path shot with someone walking through and then another one once they've left, producing two quite different images.

If you are walking with friends, you'll want those essential group shots that say 'here we are, having made it to (insert name of high pass/mountain top/final destination)'—but more interesting are the pictures of friends doing something natural like putting on boots outside a hut or talking to locals. Photographing the locals alone is another matter. I'm one of those people who shy away from photographing people who would make a wonderful subject because their lives are significantly different from mine. Let's face it, they are always poorer and living a tougher life. Occasionally I ask if I might take a photo and some decline or give half-hearted consent, so I prefer to avoid putting people through that awkwardness and I'll only ask if I've established some level of rapport. It's my loss and I'm jealous of others who have either the open personality to charm a subject or the thick hide to feel no guilt. This angst-ridden position will be more thoroughly tested when I get around to walking in countries where locals are more exotic.

I'm more at ease photographing flowers and other less self-conscious things, although a lack of awareness doesn't stop them from swaying in the breeze or bolting back into a burrow. For wildlife, a telephoto lens is indispensable. If you're keen to take detailed close-ups of plants or insects, consider adding a macro filter to your kit. Everyone sees different things along the way: Jez captured images of numerous giant slugs in an array of grey-brown hues. If you're walking with other photographers, you might be tempted to forgo an obvious shot (other than a slug) simply because others have already taken it. Don't give in to this. If a particular scene can only be taken from one vantage point, take your turn, as your composition is bound to differ. On the other hand, if there are several viewpoints, look for something other than the obvious.

Light matters

Lighting conditions change but it's worth setting camera controls and filters before you start off each day, then adjusting if necessary. Even if you're using automatic settings, you might choose a 'landscape' mode as your default, and just change to photograph people or flowers. If you're prepared to exercise a little more power and control, you might switch to a programmable mode and change the white balance as appropriate (overcast or sunny) and also select the shutter speed and/or aperture for the conditions. You should also set the ISO (a digital camera's light sensitivity) to a slow speed (say ISO 100) for clarity and detail in landscapes and only increase it if there's a risk of camera shake. When shooting wildflowers at close range or interesting rocks in the foreground, pay attention to the depth of field, changing the aperture to achieve the desired effect.

Digital cameras generally have a somewhat less dynamic range than their film predecessors and don't capture the same broad range of light and dark elements in the one picture. In scenes that are partially shadowed, sunlit areas will tend to 'blow out' and lose detail, or features in the shadows will disappear into the gloom. Canyons and coastal cliffs-and-sea are tricky, and trying to photograph them reminds me that the human eye and brain are an amazing team. Try taking several shots of the same scene, with bracketed exposures, making use of the exposure compensation control that your camera (whether compact or

SLR) probably has. In rainforest or thick woodland, low light can cause difficulties and you may have to wait until you reach a clearing by a stream or pool.

Make use of rest breaks by rivers or waterfalls to play with different shutter speeds to convey moving water, or to catch reflections in a lake when the breeze drops. It's generally accepted that the lighting in the early morning and evening offers more to photographers: the low angle is better for textures and shadows, and the light has a warmer quality. Make a sortie out from wherever you are staying to make use of these times. When you're walking in the middle of the day, look for subjects that have intrinsic interest and won't suffer too much from overhead lighting.

Post-walk work

Even if you want a straight photographic record of your walk, a little post-trip tweaking may be helpful. Altitude and summer heat create a haze and a blue colour cast that can be corrected by adjusting contrast levels and colour balance with editing software. If you're feeling cunning, scenes washed out by overly bright or flat lighting can have tones darkened by blending multiple copies of the original. If you took bracketed shots of those problem scenes with shadows and bright patches, they can be merged to make the perfect exposure. If your lens couldn't zoom in to the subject sufficiently, a little cropping will fix the problem. Some photographers will draw the line at that—fixing problems—while others will want to use the techniques available in post-production software to maximise the impact of their photos and to create artworks.

The great danger of the digital era is that you arrive home with more photographs than even you want to see. Save them all onto whatever medium is now current and then cull, cull, cull so that you have a selection of great photos. Caption these while you can remember where you were. I take reference shots of orientation tables to help me name mountain peaks and landmarks later.

Now you're in a position to print the best and put them in an album or, if you have time to lay it out, to order a personalised printed and bound book—a wonderful memento of a great walk. A digital slide show is very easy to set up for viewing on a television or computer and you can add music if people aren't interested in hearing the details of your journey. Unless your viewers are hoping to replicate your walk, there's no rule that you must show pictures in strict narrative order; the whole thing may make more sense rearranged by theme. I love looking at good images, but slide shows are considered the ultimate punishment by some, so choose your audience carefully. And remember to invite Robert Dessaix along.

KEEPING A JOURNAL

Francis Bacon thought it strange that people would keep journals on a sea voyage but omit to do so when travelling on land, where so much more is to be observed. 'Let diaries therefore be brought into use,' he decreed in 1625.

If, like mine, your memory increasingly resembles the end of a fireworks display—all smoky haze—jotting notes in a journal is something you should consider doing after each day's walk. If you're too tired and just want to tumble into the bunk after dinner, think about Douglas Mawson on his ill-fated Antarctic expedition of 1912–13; he managed to keep a detailed journal while his two companions died horrible deaths and his fingers succumbed to frostbite. If you leave it until later, precious details will have fizzled and fallen into the dark. At least jot down some notes that can be written up more fully during a rest day or on the train journey home. This is particularly important if you are walking without a partner, whether solo or as part of a group.

Even with a corroborator, there are reasons to keep a personal journal: John's memory is undoubtedly superior, but his brain does tend to store things differently to mine: at the end of a trip he can reliably recite the courses of each menu we've consumed, but won't remember a single human being we encountered.

Consider scribbling down notes about the day's walk: the terrain that your route passed over, the type of vegetation, things that raised your spirits or tested your abilities, descriptions of the settlements you passed through, and of the people you met along the way. You might impart information to others about the practicalities of a particular route, things you wish someone had told you in advance. Everyone's interests are different, of course. I recently read one walker's blog where she provided incredible detail about the power bars consumed at each break. I never knew there was such variety. You'll enjoy reading later about the quirks of your accommodation and hosts. Take care what you jot down about fellows in your own party, though; you might want to try shorthand if things get edgy. Even if you don't intend a journal to be read by others, write as if you do. It will prompt you to exercise your brain more and to avoid clichéd language.

If you are walking with friends, and you don't have any major blow-ups, you might consider sharing journals after the trip, either as a text file or a scanned image of pages. I suggest the latter because Jez kept a remarkable diary on his first trip with us that can only be fully appreciated in facsimile: every part of the page was filled with strange diagrams and the scrawl was enhanced with extravagant misspellings. It takes some work to decipher, but it's fascinating to read his fresh reactions to aspects of travel that were to us, by then, almost commonplace. Although the script wasn't copperplate, perhaps we have a nascent Wainwright in the family.

Even raw, scribbled notes can form the basis for a solid narrative, given a little massaging. At the conclusion of a walk, hindsight also allows you to add further interest: what emerged as the high point of the walk? What was unexpected? What posed the greatest challenges? Don't shy away from the unpleasant moments and don't spare the details when things didn't go according to plan; these often prove to be the most fascinating passages after sufficient time has smoothed your ruffled pride. It's no coincidence that the most entertaining travel narratives are preoccupied with the traveller's trials. Robert Louis Stevenson stumbling haplessly over the Cévennes and Bill Bryson blundering along the Appalachian Trail both cut memorable figures. It may well be that you don't use the notes for anything beyond reliving the walking experience in years to come. Then again, they could be the basis for a gripping travel book, or simply for a book on walking.

18. *Regaining civilisation*

......

The destination has been reached, the journey achieved on foot, and the pack set down for the last time. Now you can sink into your seat on the bus or train or plane with a great sense of satisfaction and perhaps a little relief. It's an odd feeling coming off the path, particularly if it has taken you somewhere relatively remote. According to Henry David Thoreau, explorers who had been travelling long on the remote steppes of Tartary reported that 'On re-entering cultivated lands, the agitation, perplexity and turmoil of civilization oppressed and suffocated us; the air seemed to fail us, and we felt every moment as if about to die of asphyxia.'

Having encouraged you to take a long walk, the last thing I would want is for you to suffocate on your return. True, the chaotic twittering of society can seem a little strange—much television appears downright surreal—and the return to normal, working life can be a touch banal after your series of constant small adventures.

There are, however, compensations: a shower where you know how the hot tap will perform; familiar cuisine; a comfortable mattress; the chance to enjoy family and friends once again. These are things that every traveller relishes on return, but the walker has the added pleasures of wearing something other than boots and of reading more than one chapter of a book before the head starts to nod. If your walk has been a lengthy one, your body may be in better condition than it has been for quite some time and you can easily conquer local challenges that you earlier considered out of your league. Indeed, your body won't appreciate an abrupt halt after a daily pattern of walking and you should make time to take it on outings, if you did not have the habit beforehand. You will probably have a healthy appetite as your body restocks, but take care not to let it overload.

You will inevitably come home to a stack of laundry, a heap of bills and megabytes of emails to answer. Despite pressing concerns, let the glow of your achievements linger awhile. Get the map out and trace your route; put a name to a few features that you passed. Do some background reading; while it would have proved useful beforehand, it will make more sense after the walk. Print off a selection of your best photographs and enjoy them. There will come a time when neither you nor I will be able to walk as far or as fast; it's important to store up some of those moments that will nourish the soul later, in Wordsworthian fashion:

For oft, when on my couch I lie
In vacant or in pensive mood,
They flash upon that inward eye
Which is the bliss of solitude;
And then my heart with pleasure fills,
And dances with the daffodils.

(FROM 'DAFFODILS')

Beyond the lasting pleasures of specific memories, your journey will probably have shifted your attitudes and changed you fundamentally. To start with, there's an element of pride in completing a walking excursion. The witty Max Beerbohm thought there was rather too much pride: 'People seem to think there is something inherently noble and virtuous in the desire to go for a walk.' He could easily have been writing about Thoreau, who, in his famous lecture on walking, expressed amazement at the 'moral insensibility' of any person who chose to stay at work or home rather than go walking.

There is a risk that walking can lead us into zealotry; this whole book could be viewed as an extended piece of partisan preaching. Sensible walkers, though, temper their enthusiasm with a measure of self-awareness. In his essay 'In Praise of Walking', Leslie Stephen confided that, on reaching a far headland on foot and eating his 'modest sandwiches', 'I have fancied myself on such occasions a felicitous blend of poet and saint—which is an agreeable sensation. What I wish to point out, however, is that the sensation is confined to the walker.' After coping with small hardships and physical challenges, a little pride is warranted and a good thing if it increases your self-confidence.

A walking excursion is a true break from civilised life and its messy complications. As far back as 1807, William Wordsworth could write of the modern condition:

> The world is too much with us; late and soon,
> Getting and spending, we lay waste our powers:
> Little we see in Nature that is ours;
> We have given our hearts away, a sordid boon!
>
> (FROM 'THE WORLD IS TOO MUCH WITH US')

The philosopher Jean-Jacques Rousseau and his followers believed the antidote to the ills of the modern world was a return to a simpler way of living. A walking excursion gives us a chance to trial the efficacy of that prescription and, for me, the paring down of life—reducing it to the basic rhythm of walking, eating and sleeping—is a great balm to the overloaded senses. It would, however, be naive for me to think that, even if my feet permitted it, I could extend this pattern indefinitely. My preferred style of walking usually involves a long flight, lodging and a quantity of good meals, all of which come at a cost which must be earned— and there we are, back in the reality of getting and spending. True, I could toughen up, put a tent in my backpack, avoid environmentally damaging transport and become more self-sufficient, but there are elements of the civilised world that my body would sorely miss. It's a matter of balance. Perhaps when we return home, we are more inclined to simplify our lives, or at least to avoid further clutter.

Spending time in the natural world rewards us with a different perspective on our lives and with altered priorities. We might even have a degree of serenity which will last until our next walking opportunity draws near. Certainly, we return more appreciative of the environment and aware of our ability to change it for the worse—and, hopefully, also for the better. An important part of a long walk is the coming home. If walking through different places and landscapes helps us to understand our own environment, we bring something home with us more worthwhile than any photographs, souvenirs or even memories.

A final word of advice, as regaining civilisation can be physically dangerous. Unless you have walked into Venice, watch out for traffic.

Perambulations

· · · · · ·

TOP TEN LISTS

When I sat down to compile a single shortlist of my favourite long walks, I was confounded, so here are my current sub-lists. If you're looking for inspiration, the following letters indicate:

A—routes that can be walked with commercial assistance

C—routes where camping is necessary

X—long-distance routes we made up ourselves.

My top ten centre-based walking areas
(in no particular order; all offer day-walks for a range of abilities)

Blue Mountains (Australia)

Vanoise Alps (France)

Ampezzo Dolomites (Italy)

Bernese Oberland (Switzerland)

High Pyrenees (France)

Yosemite National Park (USA)
Salzkammergut (Austria)
Lake District (England)
Gran Paradiso (Italy)
Sydney coastline (Australia)

My top ten long-distance walks
(in order of increasing difficulty if you're walking independently)

South West Coastal Path (England)   A
Routeburn Track (New Zealand)   A
Overland Track (Australia)   A
Rees-Dart Walk (New Zealand)
Verdon Gorge and beyond (France)
The Lycian Way (I'm an optimist!)   A
Wainwright's Coast-to-Coast (northern England)   A
Corsica, coast to mountains (Mediterranean)   X
Tour of Mont Blanc (France/Italy/Switzerland)   A
Walker's Haute Route (France/Switzerland)   A

My top ten cultural and historic walks
(in order of increasing difficulty)

Tarn Gorges (France)
Amalfi Coast day-walks (Italy)
The Ridgeway (England)   A
Hilltowns of Umbria (Italy)   X
Offa's Dyke Path (Wales)   A
Cinque Terre circuit (Italy)   X
Dordogne circuit (France)   X

Alsace and the Vosges (France)   X

High Alpujarras (Spain)   X

Way of St Jacques, Le Puy to Conques (France)   A

My top ten 'to do' walks
(for more adventurous walkers, in order of increasing difficulty)

Thorsborne Trail, Hinchinbrook Island (Australia)   C

Tongariro Circuit (New Zealand)

Isle of Skye day-walks (Scotland)

Julian Alps (Slovenia)

Jotunheimen National Park (Norway)

Dolomites traverse (Italy)   X

Torres del Paine circuit (South America)   A

The Himalaya (perhaps in Bhutan or Sikkim)   A

Skaftafell National Park (Iceland)   C

Highline Trail (USA)   C

USEFUL WEBSITES

Web addresses change faster than Italian parliaments, but here are some helpful sites that were current at the time of writing.

Walkers' organisations (with an English-language version)

- www.americanhiking.org—US hiking society
- www.bushwalking.org.au—an Australian site, with various links
- www.cai.it—Italian alpine club, with details of refuges
- www.canadatrails.ca/hiking—describes long routes in Canada
- www.dvl.dk—a Danish rambler's association
- www.era-ewv-ferp.org—European body, detailing E-paths and countries
- www.ldwa.org.uk—information on British long-distance paths
- www.pttk.pl—Poland's country-lovers' society!
- www.ramblers.org.uk—a British walking association
- www.stfturist.se—Sweden's touring club
- www.turistforeningen.no—Norway's mountain-touring club; informative

Useful walking information

- www.webwalking.com—a directory with links to sites worldwide
- www.walkingontheweb.co.uk—a directory with a focus on Europe

- www.gorp.com—a directory with a focus on North America
- www.john.chapman.name/bushwalk.html—walking in Australia by a respected writer
- www.newzealand.com/travel—NZ tourism (then search 'walking')
- www.discoverireland.ie/walking—Ireland's tourist office; detailed walks given
- www.southafrica.info—includes walking areas in South Africa
- www.trekkinginturkey.com—details two long walks in Turkey
- www.utivist.is—hiking in Iceland
- www.ont.lu/index.php—Luxembourg's tourist office; search on 'walks'

Trekking operators
- www.auswalk.com.au—guided and self-guided walks in Australia
- www.backroads.com—guided camping and inn-to-inn treks
- www.countrywalkers.com—guided walks in over thirty countries
- www.exodus.co.uk—guided treks worldwide
- www.peregrineadventures.com—guided treks worldwide
- www.sherpa-walking-holidays.co.uk—guided and self-guided walks, mainly in Europe

- www.walkingtheworld.com—treks for the over-fifties
- www.wildernesstravel.com—guided treks worldwide
- www.worldexpeditions.com—guided treks worldwide, and self-guided in Europe

Accommodation
- www.bedandbreakfast.com—B&Bs in 110 countries
- www.gites-refuges.com—French huts by route or region
- www.hostels.com—database of hostels worldwide
- www.hutten.be—mountain cabins across Europe
- www.iloveinns.com—US and Canadian B&Bs
- www.iyhf.org—international hostelling; links to national sites
- www.minshuku.jp—Japanese family-run B&Bs
- www.townandcountry.ie—Irish B&Bs (search 'activity holidays')

Also, try searching regional tourist websites for different levels of accommodation.

Rail
- www.amtrak.com—US rail
- www.nationalrail.co.uk—routes, fares and schedules in Britain
- www.raileurope.com—for thirty-five European rail systems
- www.viarail.ca—Canada rail

Books and maps

- www.stanfords.co.uk—retail online sales for walking books and maps
- www.themapshop.com.au—smaller range of walking maps; based in Australia
- www.mapsworldwide.com—smaller range of walking maps; based in USA
- www.trailblazer-guides.com—route guides for Britain and selected regions worldwide
- www.lonelyplanet.com—a series of walking guides for different countries
- www.cicerone.co.uk—numerous walking guides, mainly for Britain and Europe

FURTHER READING

Here's a selection of relevant books, arranged from the general to the specific, plus a couple that are of literary interest.

Claes Grundsten, *Trek!*, Duncan Baird, 2006; the most stunning of the recent crop of lavish big books on specific walks around the world

Jack Johnson (ed.), *Trekking Atlas of the World*, New Holland, 2006; summarises over 50 established treks worldwide

Walt Unsworth, *Classic Walks of the World*, Oxford Illustrated Press, 1985; getting old but the walks are still classics

Gillian and John Souter, *Classic Walks in Western Europe*, Off the Shelf, 2000; detailed walk notes for walks through thirteen regions

——*Walking Italy*, Off the Shelf, 2002; mainly on day-walks from a base

——*Walking France*, Off the Shelf, 2005; details mostly long walks

Adam Nicolson, *The National Trust Book of Long Walks*, Weidenfeld & Nicolson, 1981; a fascinating guide to ten of Britain's long paths

Alfred Wainwright—any of his books on walking in northern England

Kev Reynolds, *Walking in the Alps*, Cicerone, 2005; a wonderful overview of walking areas

Sven Klinge, *Classic Walks of Australia*, New Holland, 2000; includes day-walks and long walks

Craig Potton, *Classic Walks of New Zealand*, Craig Potton, 1998; plus others from this publisher

Chris Townsend, *The Advanced Backpacker*, Ragged Mountain Press, 2001; well written and specifically for wilderness walkers

Quentin and Jonathan Chester, *The Outdoor Companion*, Simon & Schuster, 1991; for wilderness walkers—with 'surviving' in the subtitle

Richard Dawood, (ed.), *Travellers' Health*, Oxford University Press, 2002; a comprehensive guide to everything nasty that can happen to you

Peter Eastway, *Landscape Travel Photography*, Lonely Planet, 2005; a brief but interesting handbook

Robert Henson, *The Rough Guide to Weather*, Rough Guides, 2007; a comprehensive guide

E.V. Mitchell, (ed.), *The Pleasures of Walking*, Vanguard, 1948; currently out of print but contains some wonderful essays on walking

Ron Strickland, (ed.), *Shank's Mare: A compendium of remarkable walks*, Paragon House, 1988; a collection of more recent literature with a walking theme

PACKING CHECKLIST
Select for expected conditions.

Footwear
- ❑ hiking boots or shoes
- ❑ evening shoes (sandals or trainers)
- ❑ hiking socks and liner socks

Clothing
- ❑ underwear/sleepwear (could be the same)
- ❑ thermal underwear (long top and leggings)
- ❑ zip-off trousers or shorts/long pants
- ❑ hiking shirt (according to climate)
- ❑ fleece jacket
- ❑ a change of clothes

Rain gear
- ❑ breathable waterproof jacket
- ❑ waterproof over-trousers

Accessories
- ❑ bandanna (for brow-mopping or bandaging)
- ❑ sunhat with brim
- ❑ warm hat and short scarf (for cold climates)
- ❑ gloves (liner/insulating/waterproof)
- ❑ swimwear (or not)
- ❑ gaiters (if expecting deep snow, mud or snakes)

Essential kit
- ❑ backpack and fold-away day-pack (or sturdy day-pack and other luggage)
- ❑ dry sack liner (a large garbage bag would suffice)
- ❑ waterproof pack cover
- ❑ stuff sacks, resealable plastic bags and a bag for rubbish
- ❑ map (with case) and compass
- ❑ water flask or hydration pack
- ❑ water purifier (tablets or filter)
- ❑ head-torch
- ❑ sunglasses (and prescription glasses)
- ❑ a waterproof watch
- ❑ a whistle
- ❑ notepad, pencil and pen
- ❑ local currency and credit/debit card
- ❑ tickets, travel insurance & passport

Useful kit
- ❑ trekking poles
- ❑ insect repellent
- ❑ notes on route, timetables & accommodation
- ❑ repair kit: tape, spare bootlace, safety pin, needle and thread
- ❑ pocket knife
- ❑ airtight food box (and lunch supplies)
- ❑ camera, bag, batteries, memory card and recharger

Toiletries

❑ microfibre towel
❑ toothbrush and toothpaste
❑ sunscreen and lip balm
❑ soap (biodegradable for outdoors)
❑ shampoo/conditioner
❑ moisturiser
❑ comb or fold-up hairbrush (or fingers)
❑ earplugs
❑ tampons and sanitary pads
❑ toilet paper or small pack of tissues
❑ nail cutters / scissors
❑ razor
❑ prescription medication

First aid kit

❑ pain relief
❑ antihistamine
❑ anti-inflammatory drug
❑ anti-diarrhoea drug
❑ antiseptic
❑ blister treatment
❑ sticking plasters
❑ crepe bandage
❑ tweezers
❑ rehydration sachets
❑ emergency blanket

Optional

❑ inner sheet, preferably silk
❑ elasticated support(s) for knee or ankle
❑ lightweight umbrella
❑ universal plug
❑ stretchy hanging line
❑ small binoculars
❑ book to read and pass on
❑ mobile phone
❑ GPS

Camping gear

❑ lightweight tent
❑ sleeping mat & sleeping bag
❑ stove, cooking pot and matches
❑ eating utensils
❑ food!

Acknowledgements

......

It is unlikely that this book would have surfaced had it not been for the enduring encouragement of Kathy Mossop, the guidance of Rebecca Kaiser and the skills of Angela Handley and the team from Allen & Unwin. It would certainly have been thinner if not for the advice and example of many walking friends and for the good company of John.

Index

......